I0158115

# AN ALPHABET OF MEN

DATING MY WAY FROM ADAM TO ZAK

SALLY MORGAN

Seabright Books
VICTORIA, BC

Copyright © 2016 by Sally Morgan.

All rights reserved. No part of this publication may be reproduced, distributed or transmitted in any form or by any means, including photocopying, recording, or other electronic or mechanical methods, without written permission of the publisher, except by a reviewer, who may quote brief passages.

Published in Canada by Seabright Books
1945 Lands End Road
North Saanich, BC V8L-5J2

Cover design by Andy Ugro
Book Layout ©2016 BookDesignTemplates.com

Publisher's Note: This is a work of creative nonfiction. I have recreated events and conversations from my memories of them. Mistakes and inaccuracies are mine. I have changed the names and sometimes the identifying details of many of the individuals in this book in order to protect their privacy.

Book Layout ©2013 BookDesignTemplates.com

An Alphabet of Men / Sally Morgan
ISBN 978-0-9958436-0-8

*For Jerome*
*for risking your heart and protecting mine*

# PROLOGUE

The woman leans over the table toward me, peering intently at my right hand, lying open in hers. "This line," she says, tracing her finger across my palm, "is your brain line. Do you see the way it branches at the end? This is typical of writers." She looks up at me. "Do you write?"

I'm in a shopping mall of all places, sitting across a little table from a palm reader. I observe her with interest, this woman who could pass for a school secretary; she looks far more ordinary than I would have imagined. It's September and the cool of the mall is a welcome relief from the late-summer heat outside. Behind us, people rush past, hurrying to complete quick lunchtime errands. I'm vaguely aware of music playing in the background. But the busy environment falls away as she continues. I tell her that yes, I write.

"It's only just beginning for you," she tells me.

I've never done something like this before, and I have to admit to some skepticism. But I've always been intrigued and in the last few weeks, in the way that serendipity works, I've had a number of people suggest I have my astrological chart done or that I investigate Tarot.

In our half hour session, the palm reader identifies my interest in other cultures, in art, and architecture; she can see that there has been and will continue to be lots of travel in my life; she predicts I'll be taking an educational trip at the end of October, not knowing that I'm already booked to attend a conference in New Orleans; and she tells me I've inherited much in my nature and my talents from my father. My initial skepticism quickly dissipates.

Near the end of the session, she turns to matters of the heart. Running her finger along my right index finger, she asks, "Do you see how the top part of this finger curves in? That shows you were deeply disappointed in a first mating, usually a marriage."

I'm not sure that disappointed quite sums up that experience. Shocked? Shaken? Knocked flat? My former husband walked out of our seventeen-year marriage with little warning and with even less empathy. We had three small boys at home and my father had just been diagnosed with terminal cancer. The timing wasn't exactly ideal. Disappointed? Absolutely.

The palm reader makes a number of other quite astute – and not very flattering – observations about my ex-husband and then moves on. She looks carefully at the side of my hand, below my little finger. Then she pulls out a magnifying glass to take a closer look, as though she's seen something unexpected. "There are quite a few men here," she says, sounding a bit surprised. Or is it shocked? I do a quick calculation about how many men I've dated in the past six months. I'm up to about twenty. And if I think of all the men I've dated in the five years since my divorce, that number would be closer to forty. Most of these dates have been one-off coffee dates, but still. Forty.

Yes, that is quite a few men.

She gazes at me in a disconcerting way. "A huge theme for you," the woman tells me, "is protection. You're protecting somebody right now who is vulnerable. You're really worried about them."

My children? I've been thinking recently about the ways in which I've protected them since the divorce, often at the expense of my love life. My three boys, all still school-age, have been my first priority and though I've managed to squeeze in all those dates, it's been in the corners of a busy life, on weekends and evenings when the boys have been at their dad's house. In five years, I've introduced them to one man, the one guy with whom I had a longer-term relationship. But when they've been with me, the boys have come first.

But she isn't talking about my kids; she's talking about me. "You have a childlike heart," she tells me. I feel tears well up and the sudden urge to flee. This is not a conversation I want to have with a palm reader, especially in a shopping mall.

She looks at me kindly. "It's a good thing. You see the good in the world, the wonder. There is no bitterness or pessimism. But your heart is about five years old. You have to protect it."

Protect my heart. I'd like to tell you that this is news to me, but it's not. I've been hearing much the same message from my therapist since my divorce. That trusting, childlike heart of mine has been broken wide open three times in five years. In five years, I've lost three important men in my life: my dad, my ex-husband, and most recently, the one man I'd dated long-term since my divorce. During our time together, Griff had restored my faith in love, and when he ended the relationship, I'd been left shaken and lost.

Really, it's no wonder that I might be protecting my heart a little at this point.

I thank the palm reader and stand to leave, but she grabs my hand, stopping me. She leans across the table, looking at me with concern. "The really important question you need to ask yourself about any man is whether he is somebody who will protect you, no matter what."

I'm not sure if this advice is part of what she's seen in my hand or whether it's just sensible advice from one woman to another. Either way, I leave with all kinds of things to think about, and my childlike heart, open to the mysteries of the world, is a little less skeptical.

Nine months before my visit to the palm reader, my relationship with Griff ended. After two and a half years together, he came over to my place one night and told me he was leaving. He wanted somebody he could build a life with. Though we had a passionate connection, we both knew that moving in together would never work for us. It was in the aftermath of my relationship with Griff, as I processed my grief and confusion, that I had a terrifying realization: I was going to have to endure another round of online dating. I'd been there before. And frankly, heartbreak I could deal with. Another round of Internet dating? Not so much.

I was filled with despair at the thought of facing, once again, that cycle of hope, budding excitement and then the inevitable disappointment. I'd have to muster my bright and shiny coffee-date self, over and over again and send out all those diplomatic notes to men I wasn't interested in, cheerful, airy messages with a dark subtext: "No. Never. Not if you were the last man on earth."

Anyway, there I was, reeling from the end of a relationship and in no fit state to start dating again. But at that point, in my mid-forties, I knew a few things about myself. I absolutely knew that even though I was pretty good at single, I was meant to be in a long-term, stable relationship. I wasn't ready yet, but at some point, I wanted to find a man who I could invite into my whole life and with whom I might craft a life-long relationship. Eventually I was going to have to date again.

What would be the compelling way to approach this dreaded task?

I learned the value of finding the compelling way during my divorce. There are few things worse than online dating, but one of them is getting a divorce. I mean, how can you possibly make an experience like that fun?

One possibility is to agree to have your divorce filmed for national television, which is what my ex-husband and I did.

It's a long story.

My ex and I had gone to a lawyer together to find out about collaborative divorce. A day later a television producer contacted that lawyer and asked her if she knew of any couples that might agree to have their collaborative divorce filmed. For national television. Why yes! Of course she did!

Any sensible woman in my position would have said no. But sensible has never been one of my virtues.

Okay, I realize that being in a documentary about divorce might not be the most compelling way through divorce for everyone, but it worked for me. Instead of sitting with my lawyer in a dreary boardroom somewhere, feeling angry with my ex-husband and sorry for myself, I found myself in a hip, light-filled high-rise in downtown Vancouver. I had people fussing over me, I had cameras rolling, and, best of all, I had diva lights. I just can't explain to you how truly beautiful diva lights are. The first time those lights came on and the cameras rolled, I realized I'd missed my calling: I was meant to be a weather girl.

I was in my element! I was still deeply hurt that my ex-husband had left me and angry at him for tearing our family apart; I had no confidence that I'd find love again; and I was really scared about my future. But instead of feeling sorry for myself, I was worrying about whether I had chosen the right shade of lipstick and if I should have chosen a sedate beige sweater rather than something cheerful and pink. And if all those lights and cameras and fussing weren't enough, the lawyers were high-profile Vancouver lawyers, so every time we had a session, I was whisked across the water from my Vancouver Island home by helicopter.

I know.

This is what it means to be a celebrity. And, having had my fifteen minutes of fame, I can tell you this: I could do it again.

The compelling way. How could I make the prospect of dating more enticing?

I thought about my dating experiences the last time round, the crazy messages I'd received and the unusual characters I'd met. And I had to admit that, while the actual dates were often disheartening, there was something interesting or funny in every encounter. The last time I'd been online dating, I'd been the darling of the dinner party circuit. All my safely married friends knew that they could count on me for an entertaining story about one recent dating misadventure or another.

One of my favourite stories was about Lawrence of the Five White Evils. Lawrence had a Zen-like aura, a laid-back, totally chill approach to life and to dating. At least that was what I had decided, based on his brief profile and the occasional messages he'd send, messages that would breeze into my inbox weeks apart.

"Hey! Sitting here sipping on some rosehip tea and breathing in the divine spirit of this amazing afternoon. Hope you're having an equally sacred day."

I'd get these messages after I'd rushed home from work, after I'd raced my three boys around from one after-school activity to the next, after I'd cooked dinner, cleaned the kitchen and put everyone to bed. It was hard to identify anything particularly sacred or divine in my day. But his messages kept floating in from time to time.

Then one day, he invited me out for coffee. Actually he suggested herbal tea.

"Hey! I'm going to be out in your neck of the woods tomorrow afternoon. Not sure if you're around, but it would be great to meet you. Is there a quiet coffee shop somewhere out that way where we could grab a pot of tea?"

Normally, I didn't meet a guy for coffee unless we'd been chatting regularly and I had a pretty good sense of who he was. I hardly knew anything about Lawrence except that he was deeply interested in holistic healing and was heading out soon to attend a month-long spiritual retreat. But there was something so laid back, so flaky, so harmless about Lawrence, that against my better judgment, I agreed to meet him.

He strolled into the coffee shop completely serene and completely oblivious, it seemed, to the fact that he'd already kept me waiting for ten minutes. I was already feeling deeply not serene. "Hey!" he drawled, a beatific smile spreading across his face. He dropped his lanky body down into an armchair across from me and gazed over at my latte. "You've got a drink already. I'll just be a sec while I get some tea."

I watched him head to the counter to order. He was dressed in all natural, probably organic, and very rumpled clothes, and he was wearing Birkenstocks. Now I love my Birkenstocks. Don't get me wrong. But I had the distinct impression that he might only own earthy looking sandals. "He's heading off on a spiritual retreat," I reminded myself. "You're just having coffee. Nobody says you have to marry the guy." (This last part, by the way, was one of my dating mantras: it's just coffee; nobody says you have to marry the guy. I found that it was a very effective way to talk myself down and avoid bolting half way through a meeting).

As I watched Lawrence return to our corner of the coffee shop, a pot of tea and mug in hand, I took a deep breath, recovering from my pique at his tardiness. I smiled my most charming smile and said, "So tell me about your retreat. It sounds fascinating."

Yep. I've got the bright and shiny coffee-date thing down cold.

So Lawrence told me about his retreat and his commitment to yoga and how he was meditating an hour every morning. I smiled and nodded, adding a brief comment here and there, well aware that retreats and hour-long daily yoga sessions were not ever going to be a part of my single-mother reality and wondering why I had agreed to meet a man who was clearly so unsuitable for me.

Taking my polite nods and comments as encouragement, Lawrence moved on from meditation to whole foods. It took me a while to notice that his serenity was, almost imperceptibly turning to quiet conviction. But as I reached for my latte, I saw his eyes narrow. "Most people do not understand at all about The Five White Evils," he said, looking at my drink meaningfully. I felt myself sit up a little straighter, my dating hackles activated. I'm not really one for calling anything evil. Especially with those implied capital letters. His voice gained power, at first in a way that was a little embarrassing. "They don't know how dangerous it is to consume milk," he declared. As I put my latte back on the table, he continued. "Milk is poison," he stated, his eyes bulging just a little.

Drawing away from him, I smiled gently and said in my calmest voice, "Everything in moderation, right?"

I don't think he even heard me. "And white sugar," he declared, "is even worse." Now a vein on his neck was bulging and his voice was reaching an alarming volume. At this point, I'd pulled as far away from him as I could and was holding on to the arms of my chair. "People don't understand the danger of consuming salt!" The quiet conviction was fast approaching hysterical fanaticism.

And I was pushing myself out of my chair, smiling in a way that I hoped would assure him that this whole conversation was really cool with me, but that I'd suddenly remembered a pressing prior engagement.

He didn't seem to notice. "And white flour!" He was shouting now.

I've always regretted that I didn't have the courage to stick around to find out what the Fifth White Evil was. Rice? Cauliflower? Cocaine? It's been nagging at me for years.

So that was Lawrence, and if there is any wisdom for you to take away from my crazy coffee date, it's this: screen your dates carefully, people! Screen your dates and always have a rock-solid excuse for why you can't possibly see somebody a second time.

About two years after I met Lawrence of the Five White Evils for that ill-fated latte, he tracked me down through my work and sent me another breezy email. I promise you, I am not making any of this up.

"Hey! Sorry not to get back to you sooner, but I really had fun meeting you and wondered if you'd like to get together for another cup of tea?"

Two years later?

When I showed the message to my girlfriend, who had heard the story about Lawrence of the Five White Evils, she laughed, and then gave me some excellent advice: "Tell him you're married and are expecting twins."

You see what I mean? Online dating is not for the faint of heart.

So, let's get back to that problem of how to make another round of dating compelling. I decided that if I was going to have to go through this ordeal once more, then I might as well tell those stories. And so I began a blogging project I called *An Alphabet of Men*, with the plan to start with *A is for Adam* and to date my way as far into the alphabet as was necessary. I planned to chronicle my dating experiences, tame and tawdry, and to share the lessons I learned along the way. I hoped that in the process I might heal my child-like heart and find somebody who I knew would truly protect it.

And I was confident that this would all happen somewhere well before I'd have to meet *Z is for Zak*.

# ONE

# WHEN FAIRY TALES END

The ending, when it comes, is at once unexpected and inevitable. As rain falls heavily in the winter darkness outside, Griff sits in my living room, holding both my hands in his. "I love you, Baby," he says, holding my gaze. "But I can't do this any longer."

I'm silent, shocked by the sudden announcement. Only yesterday, we'd spent the day laughing and clowning together, creating a promotional video for his construction business. There'd been no tension, no iciness, nothing to suggest an imminent break up. Even though I'm surprised, I'm resigned. In some part of me, I've been expecting this for ages, knowing that sooner or later our differences would tear us apart.

Griff explains how much pressure he's feeling in launching a new business, how little time he has had for himself. And then he gets to the heart of it: "In the end," he says, "you've never let me fully into your life." The statement hits me with the force of absolute truth. I haven't. And I know I never will.

From the beginning, I've shielded my three boys from Griff. At first, I wanted to protect them from the possibility of connecting and then potentially losing another important adult in their lives. They'd had to endure the pain of their parents' divorce, and then shortly after, the death of their beloved grandad. I didn't want them to experience any further loss.

Once Griff and I knew one another better, I began to see how different our parenting philosophies were, and found another reason to maintain distance. Griff had four beautiful and very well behaved children. He only saw them for a weekend every month, because they lived in another city, but I could see when they visited how much they loved him and wanted to please him. He was a loving and fun dad, but he parented with an authoritarian bent that worried me; in turn, he found my more relaxed parenting style troubling and was convinced that unless I was much stricter, my boys were going to cause all kinds of trouble as they got older.

Griff holds my hand and looks into my eyes as he talks. "We've been together nearly three years now, and we still can't figure out how to move in together."

A part of me wants to protest and make promises. But we both know that moving in would be disastrous. The parenting is just the tip of the iceberg. Griff is a perfectionist, whereas I live by the motto, *Good enough!* His house is always five-star hotel clean. A better analogy for mine would be youth hostel. He thinks that reading a good book or spending an afternoon writing is time wasted. These activities are as elemental for me as breathing. His idea of an adventure is to stay in a nice hotel in Vegas. I want to trek in the Himalayas. And yet, for all our differences, we have such fun together and share such a strong physical connection that splitting up seems inconceivable.

In order to make things work, we've lived separate lives. When my boys are with me, I'm fully engaged with their lives, spending evenings juggling the many demands of the single mother. In those weeks, Griff comes over some evenings, but not until the boys are nearly ready for bed. He leaves again in the mornings before they are up. When the boys are with their dad, I spend most of my time at Griff's house, living in an alternate reality.

Griff looks at me sadly. "I just want to be able to wake up every morning with someone."

That someone he's talking about is not going to be me.

Griff stands to leave. "I should go." I nod again, having hardly said a word. At the door he pulls me into his arms and we hold each other a long time, both of us crying. He looks down at me and whispers, "Promise me you won't ever settle." Then he kisses me, and heads out into the rain. I stand at the door and watch him back down the driveway, thinking about how hard it's going to be to let him go.

Despite our differences, our relationship had "Fairy tale" stamped all over it. I'd met Griff online, calling him into my life with a carefully written profile. It began like this:

*I can't resist a man who laughs. Can't resist someone who knows how to say yes to life. I love a man who is happy in his life and who has learned a few things along the way. I love a man who knows how to kiss a woman's shoulders.*

The universe delivered. Griff strode into my life, a powerful man, whose confidence and charm were captivating. He was a man who laughed, who absolutely knew how to say yes to life, and who knew a thing or two about kissing a woman's shoulders. He'd call me and send texts throughout the day just to tell me he loved me, or pull up in his shiny red sports car, halfway through my workday, just so he could give me a kiss. He'd take me dancing and we'd lose ourselves, forgetting that there was anyone else on the dance floor. We shared a passionate bond.

Two years after a divorce that had left me reeling and questioning my worth, I was ready for someone who would sweep me off my feet. When I met him, I wasn't looking for someone to fit into my whole life. I didn't care if my friends or my mother or my children would like this man. I picked Griff just for me. Two years out of a long marriage, I wasn't ready yet to fully invite someone into my life. I wanted intimacy, love, romance, and fun. And no complications. I'm pretty sure that Griff, who had been divorced about the same amount of time, wanted exactly the same thing. I used to describe my time with Griff as "Cinderella time." It was time so far removed from my real life that it was magical.

The universe had delivered a man I couldn't resist, which is lovely while everything is working. But it's hell on wheels when you break up.

The week that Griff and I break up, I'm on my own. My three boys are staying at their dad's. Those first lonely days are wrenching. I spend hours curled up in bed crying, grieving not just the end of the relationship, but the other big losses I've endured in the past few years. I've moved on after my divorce, but I'm still really sad to have lost my sense of family. Nothing was more important to me. And I don't think I've yet grieved the loss of my father. His death came too soon after my divorce. In those early days after Griff and I split up, I feel completely adrift and overwhelmed.

But after a few days, I start to surface from my sadness. Though I've endured these losses, I've also survived them, and I know that I'll get through this too. I begin writing about the blessings of my relationship with Griff, knowing this will be the first step in letting it go. But that makes me so sad that I alternate with lists of all the reasons why Griff was not the right man for me.

I share these reasons with my girlfriends, who gather around me, taking me for coffee and long walks, letting me talk and cry my way through my sadness. For the most part, they are sympathetic, letting me share all the reasons he wasn't right for me without saying much, and then agreeing with me that Griff had all kinds of good qualities too. Only Helen dares to share an alternate perspective.

"I liked Griff," she says, as the two of us walk through a local park after work one day. "And I'm sorry that you've broken up. But really, Sally, is this such a surprise?"

I look at her, a little startled. I'd count Helen among the most diplomatic of my friends. But I know where she's going.

"He's already done this to you once." She pauses to let the truth sink in. Griff had left me once before, about eight months after we started going out. At the time it had seemed completely out of the blue; but he admitted that he'd panicked and asked me to give him a second chance. At the time, I vowed to myself that there would be no third chance.

"And look at his pattern," Helen adds. "He left his children and moved to another city." This is also true. And it's one of the things about Griff that I struggled with from the beginning, never understanding a decision like that.

"It shouldn't be a surprise that he's ended things," Helen says gently. "He's a man who will always put his own needs first."

I get together with my friend Matt during that first week too. Matt and I met online, six months before I met Griff. Matt is a writer, and he and I had a crazy, adrenaline-soaked week of email communication that was dizzying in its playfulness. As the week progressed, the emails got longer and more flirtatious, until one night, Matt sent me this terse message: "We have to meet before this gets any further out of hand." Indeed.

It was only as I was driving into town to meet Matt for the first time that I really started to think about how different we were. I was a super-conventional, mini-van driving suburban mother of three children, who liked her wine and an occasional good steak, and who thought vanilla was a flavour of ice cream. Matt, on the other hand, was a bike-riding vegan with a professional interest in BDSM, who didn't drink at all and who had decided early on that he didn't want kids.

It took us about five minutes to realize how unsuitable we would be as a couple. And how much we liked each other anyway. We quickly became good friends, and whenever we got together, we would share stories about our latest online dating disasters. Later, once we'd both found partners, we'd dissect our respective relationships.

Matt probably knows more about my relationship with Griff than anyone except my therapist. So he's the perfect person to hash things out with now. "We were just too different," I say, trying to sound convincing. "Even if the kids weren't such an issue, there were so many other things." I list his perfectionism, his politics and his focus on money. Then I remember something that I know will make Matt laugh. "He actually had a business book written by Donald Trump!"

Matt laughs, but his specialty is to ask the hard questions. "Then why are you such a mess?"

"I still miss him!" I'm on the defensive immediately.

"But what is it that you miss? What was he giving you that you aren't giving yourself?"

That second question silences me. All at once, I see I've done it again. I've put my happiness in the hands of a man. When I met Griff, I was so busy, I hardly had time for him. My summer was booked solid with camping trips with my kids, a writing retreat, and a sailing trip in Greece. I was writing, dancing and spending time with friends; I was eating well, doing yoga and getting massage. When I met Griff, I was taking really good care of myself.

Somewhere in the last couple of years, I've let many of those things slip. I've put all my energy into loving Griff, forgetting to look after myself. I think about the last few days. When have I even made myself a decent meal? Not once. If I'd had the boys with me, or if Griff had been in my life still, I would have cooked something healthy every night. But when it was just me? I couldn't be bothered.

Even worse, I'd started relying on Griff to make me feel loved. In fairness, he was really good at it. But I'd somehow forgotten that it was my job to make me happy, my job to make sure I feel fulfilled.

And now without Griff, I was, as Matt had so kindly pointed out, a mess. "I guess it's time to get back on the self-love wagon," I admit.

Matt gives me a wicked grin. "It's probably your only option for a while."

Later that week I get in to see my therapist, Linda. She's seen me through a divorce, and through the ups and downs of my relationship with Griff. I feel composed as I enter her office, but within minutes, I'm sobbing, barely able to talk. I share my story, but it's jumbled together with my sadness about my dad and my divorce and all the other things I'm still carrying around.

She lets me cry and listens as I tell her about the ending with Griff. But when I tell her what a shock this has been, she stops me.

"Sally, you were here less than a month ago debating whether or not to end your relationship."

How quickly I forget.

Griff had been slowly withdrawing, adding more to his schedule, and leaving less time for me. I'd seen Linda a couple of times simply to get a handle on my growing anxiety. And then over the holidays, he'd been really distant, choosing to spend Christmas Day on his own rather than coming over to my place.

"There were lovely, good things about your relationship," Linda assures me. "But it wasn't always a healthy one."

"I guess I knew that," I admit. "But why couldn't I let him go?"

Linda smiles, indicating that I know the answer already.

"I was too scared," I say. "He was so good to me and we had such amazing chemistry. I was afraid of losing that."

Linda just smiles sympathetically and waits for me to continue.

I'm starting to feel uncomfortable. "And I figured it was better to have Griff in my life on a part-time basis than not at all."

"Why is that, do you think?"

I take a deep breath before I answer. "Because I don't really believe I can find someone to share my whole life with." I sit with this for a moment. Where has that come from?

Linda says quietly, "You can."

I want to believe her. But I don't know if it's true.

"What feels true right now is that there's something wrong with me. Men leave me. My ex-husband. My dad. And now Griff."

"You know that isn't true, Sally."

"What I know is that the thing I want most – to share my whole life with somebody, kids and all – what I want most is never going to happen."

Linda watches me thoughtfully. "You are a complete package, Sally. You're beautiful and talented. It might not feel like it right now, but you're a pretty together woman."

"I think it's a bit early for *Plenty of Fish*," I say, trying to lighten the mood.

Linda laughs. "You're not ready yet, but eventually you will be. And when you're ready, you'll discover that there are good men out there who would love to be part of your whole life."

As that first week draws to a close, I can hardly wait to see my boys. I miss their crazy, lovable energy, and the house feels big and empty without them. Beyond that, I know that once they're back, I won't have time to feel sorry for myself. There are meals to prepare, homework to supervise, bedtimes to orchestrate. It's the middle of soccer and volleyball season for Gavin, David is back and forth to karate, and Luke has swimming lessons. Though I'm often exhausted by the craziness of our schedule, right now I welcome it.

The boys come barrelling into the house, their dad trailing behind with a stack of duffel bags. "Hi love," I say to David, as he reaches out to hug me.

"Hi Mom," he says, hugging me tight. At fifteen, he towers over me, but he's still my first-born, and today I hug him a little tighter than usual. Luke, who's only eight, grabs me around the waist.

"Hi, little guy," I say, hugging him too.

Gavin, who's twelve and nearly as tall as me now, waits so he can have a hug all to himself. "Hello, my love," I say, grateful for the love and affection from all three of my boys. "It's so nice to have you all home."

After the boys say goodbye to their dad, and take their things upstairs, I follow Randall out onto the porch and share my news.

He's sympathetic. "I'm sorry. It's tough, hey?"

I nod, not sure when my ex-husband and I reached a point where we could be sympathetic about our respective relationships ending.

"Griff seemed like a good guy," Randall adds. "The boys seemed to like him."

I wait until after dinner, and share the news with each of my boys separately. David, who helps me with the dishes after dinner, just leans over and gives me a half-hug. "That's too bad, Mom. I'm sorry." If truth be told, he doesn't look or sound particularly sorry.

When I tell Luke, he is equally nonplussed, and at 8 he takes the news in, and then promptly changes the subject.

It's only Gavin who is emotional. As I tell him, I see his eyes well up. He leans over and hugs me for a long minute, and I think he's really sad. I feel myself starting to cry. But then he says, "Are you okay?" He's worried about me, which of course, makes me cry even harder.

Once the boys are in bed, I spend some time writing. It's sobering for me to see how little connection my boys actually had with Griff, how little the news of our separation seems to worry them. Good learning, I think.

The only other person I need to talk to is my mother. Since Dad died, I've felt like we have to be extra careful with her. I don't want her worrying about me or the boys. But when I tell her that Griff and I have broken up, her response is succinct: "I'm sorry. Sal," she says briskly. "But I never liked him much anyway."

Okay, so here's an important dating tip: do not break up with the man in your life if he is also a contractor and finishing a renovation on your house. This is the uncomfortable situation in which Griff and I find ourselves at the end of our relationship. Fortunately, the work is almost done, and doesn't require Griff to be out at my house every day.

But I have to see him from time to time and talk on the phone with him regularly. The phone calls are awful. Every time I hear his warm, deep voice, I feel desolate. But having to see him is even worse. Today he swings by work so that I can sign some paperwork.

I see him pulling into the back parking lot, so I head outside to meet him. I'm trying to look calm, but my heart is pounding and my hands are shaking.

"Hey," he says, smiling as he steps out of his truck. He must have come from a business meeting and is dressed in jacket and tie. He looks impossibly handsome. It's all I can do not to reach out and touch him. I stand there, smiling, hardly hearing what he's saying, willing myself: "Do not touch! Do not touch!"

I sign the paperwork and hand it back to him.

"Are you doing okay?" he asks.

I nod. "Given the circumstances. How about you?"

He gives me a rueful smile. "Not so great. Awful actually."

Immediately, I start crying.

"Hey," he says, and hugs me. "I'm sorry. It's just so hard not being with you."

I want to stay there touching him forever, but I pull away. "You're not making it any easier." I walk away, but with every step, my body aches with loss.

I seek out a friend in her office, close the door and burst into tears. She is sympathetic, as always, listening as I tell her about the interaction I've just had with Griff. "You guys have that chemical thing going on," she says.

"What do you mean?" I ask.

"You had such an intense physical connection; your bodies were producing all kinds of feel-good chemicals every day. You're dealing with withdrawal along with everything else."

I think about this. "It feels that way."

"You're both addicted. It's just going to be way harder to get over each other. Time and distance. That's all that's going to help"

"Can't it just be over?" I laugh, tears streaking my face. "Can't it just be three months from now? I hate going through this!"

She smiles and leans toward me from behind her desk. "Do you know how lucky you are? I know it feels crappy right now. But lots of people never get what you had."

I start crying again. I think about Griff's hands on my body, the electric charge I felt every time he touched me.

"Griff let you see yourself as beautiful and desirable. That's a powerful thing. You didn't know that when your marriage ended."

She's right. And though I'm still sad, though my body still aches, and though I look like hell after all the tears, I leave her office feeling a little bit better. "I'm beautiful," I say to myself, trying out the idea.

It doesn't work. I'm not feeling beautiful at all. I'm drawn and tired, my eyes are bloodshot from the tears, and my makeup is ruined. But I keep going. "I'm desirable." Still nothing.

I say the words again slowly, trying to believe them. "I'm beautiful and desirable." Nothing. At least not right now.

But somewhere down the road, it might be a message I can work with.

Every ending is also a new beginning. I keep trying to remember this in the early days after Griff and I break up. I remind myself that I have to let go of this relationship to make space for what I really want and need in my life. But honestly? What I really want is to drown myself in a vat of Cosmopolitans.

The early days are bleak. They don't feel like the beginning of anything. There's no sense of hopefulness, no sense yet of possibility. Mostly, it just feels like a big, black ending. The End.

But I know I'll be okay. I've survived break ups before. In fact, I'm getting to be kind of an expert at the whole break up thing. Which is not really something I'm all that happy about.

It's at times like these that I am super grateful to be a single mom and a working professional. Mostly I used to feel kind of jealous of the stay-at-home moms I would see picking up their children after school, all calm blue ocean, still dressed in their yoga outfits, healthy meals bubbling away in the slow cookers in immaculately clean kitchens.

I, on the other hand, would be the mom racing onto the playground fifteen minutes late, completely distracted, wondering simultaneously how I could have forgotten to make that critical phone call before I flew out of work and also what the hell I was going to feed the kids before we'd have to be back out the door in an hour for soccer practice.

But in the throes of a break up, I remember how fortunate I am to be so busy. I might have very little time in my life for yoga, or healthy meals, or going to the bathroom even, but on the bright side there really isn't time in my life to get all weepy and maudlin either.

Life, I have learned, goes on. And the morning school bus waits for no child.

I'm also really grateful for my girlfriends. When my marriage ended, I realized how truly wonderful my closest friends were. They circled the wagons and took amazing care of me. About a week after my ex-husband moved out of the house, a group of them arrived with wine and party food, and a plan to cheer me up. One of them brought a chocolate-hazelnut torte, a dessert we usually couldn't eat because of my ex's hazelnut allergy. I didn't realize the symbolism until somebody else referred to it as *The Cake of Death*. Good friends indeed.

During the divorce, my girlfriends kept me busy and kept me laughing. One friend said to me, "I have two words for you, girlfriend: bikini wax. I know you're sad right now, but a year from now, you'll be having hot new-relationship sex and the rest of us will still be having boring old married-sex. Bikini wax, sister. The rest of us will be so jealous of you." At the time, she had me laughing through my tears. But she was right: a year later, the sex was hot and new and fabulous.

Hope is a wonderful thing.

And girlfriends? Even better. Even in this dark place in my life, I know that I'll be able to count on them again, that in the weeks ahead, they'll be there to check in, to offer a hug, and to offer lovely distractions. They'll be there to make me laugh and to provide wise advice.

# TWO

# DANCING TO MY OWN ALGORITHMS

Valentine's Day rolls around and I am feeling particularly blue, remembering my day with Griff the year before.

We'd spent our evening making a Valentine's dinner together and dancing to the playlist he made for the occasion. Late in the evening, he sat me down and said, "Close your eyes, baby. Don't open them until I tell you, okay?" Eyes closed, I could hear him running up and down the stairs and moving furniture. "What on earth are you up to?" I asked, laughing.

Silence.

Then I heard the first strains of "Save a Horse, Ride a Cowboy." Griff was a Calgary boy, and "Ride a Cowboy" his signature tune. As soon as I heard the opening, I knew exactly what he'd planned. I opened my eyes to see him, in jeans and a dress shirt, his head tipped forward, with one hand resting on a red suede cowboy hat. He had the male-stripper stance down cold.

As the song started, he tilted his head up, gave me a saucy smile, and started dancing. He'd clearly gone to a lot of trouble. His moves were choreographed; he'd tracked down the red hat, and he'd even found a strobe light. He strutted his way through the song, removing his clothes until he was down to just the hat. I was laughing so hard that tears were running down my face.

Forget the flowers and the chocolates! Hands down, that dance was one of the best gifts I'd ever received.

And so Valentine's Day this year isn't quite the same. I've been thinking about that dance, about the great lengths that Griff went to just to make me laugh. I feel so grateful to have had that delicious moment in my life, and today I am feeling really sad that I no longer have my very own, personal male stripper.

It's hard not to sink into a funk, and make myself believe that I'll never, ever find another man who would do something like that for me. But then I think about the brief, intense fling I had the summer after my divorce. Andrew was a research scientist who lived in Vancouver, a nice, safe four-hour journey away. Between visits, he'd write me eloquent love letters. With a fountain pen! Even now, I still get faint thinking about those letters.

When our summer romance ended, I remember thinking, "Where am I going to find another man who'll write me love letters? In fountain pen?"

And then I met Griff. For all his prowess on the dance floor, Griff was not a writer. And you know what?

It didn't matter one little bit. There were so many other lovely and good things about him that I didn't need handwritten letters. I didn't even think about handwritten letters.

So today, I bravely try to remember that I will meet someone else and there will be lovely gifts in that relationship. And instead of spending a lonely and sad Valentine's watching Netflix, I am out for dinner with Kira, who I like to refer to as The Queen of All the Internet Dating. Kira is the sort of friend who leaves lasagne on your doorstep when you're first separated; she leaves flowers for your birthday; and today she has turned down three different Valentine's Day suitors to spend the evening with me.

"You know the worst part about breaking up with Griff?" I tell her. "I'm going to have to go back to Internet dating."

"You love online dating," she laughs. "You were my inspiration to get on the Internet in the first place. Have you forgotten how much fun you had?"

"All I remember was that I had to kiss an awful lot of Internet frogs," I moan. "I don't know if I can do it again."

"When you're ready, it'll be okay," she assures me. "And I'll send you a list of the men you definitely want to avoid. I think I've dated just about all of the eligible men in Victoria."

She pauses. "Actually I'm pretty sure I've dated a couple that weren't eligible too."

One of Kira's other friends once accused her of being a serial dater. But it's one of the things I admire about her. She has an amazing capacity for juggling men. It's never been one of my talents.

"For sure," she starts, "you want to avoid the Cow Whisperer. He lives out this way." I remember her telling me about the man she dated who spent an evening rhapsodizing about the pleasures of artificially inseminating his cows. They really do use a turkey baster.

"And definitely give the Horny Baptist a miss." That was the guy who was on his best behaviour until the minute the lights went down at the movie theatre.

By now Kira and I are both giggling. "And you only date local, so you're unlikely to connect with Mushroom Man." Mushroom Man, I recall, is a botanist from the States. She pulls out her phone. "Check out this lovely selfie," she says, showing me a picture of an erect penis, which the botanist has thoughtfully sent her way.

We are way past giggling now, and into loud guffaws. The people in the restaurant are looking at us warily.

"Who would ever think that was a good idea?" I ask, laughing.

She shakes her head, as bewildered by this behaviour as I am. "But, come on, Sally! How can you not think online dating is fun when you have suitors like him?"

Kira and I spend the evening laughing about the perils of Internet dating, reminiscing about some of our particularly memorable dating moments, and coming up with the design for our own Internet dating site. And as we laugh at the place we've found ourselves, I feel my despair about the prospect of dating dissipating.

Under the despair, I feel a faint glimmer of something else, something I'm not quite ready to admit to, something that feels a little bit like excitement.

Because I'm beginning to remember that secretly I kind of like online dating.

I know. This isn't really something you're supposed to admit. But the truth is that there are aspects of online dating that are pretty addictive. I love coming up with a creative name and tagline, a sassy new profile. I love choosing just the right pictures and engaging in the playful, flirty messages back and forth. And after a breakup, there is nothing like launching a new profile and watching your inbox fill, almost immediately, with messages. It's a potent reminder that you are still attractive, still desirable. After you've had your heart broken? That's a good thing.

Beyond the attention, I love the sheer possibility in this activity. I'm an optimist by nature, the sort of woman who could see the potential in a man ten years younger, who lives 200 miles away and who races sled dogs in the winter. "Yeah! That could work," I think, noticing that he likes to read. The next thing, I'd be firing off a message before I could come to my senses and remember how little I like long-distance *anything* and how much I truly hate the cold.

By the end of my evening with Kira, my heart feels lighter and I am actually feeling okay about getting out there again. But it's early days yet. I'm not ready. I need to get over Griff. And he needs to get over me too.

"It doesn't sound like it's over between you two," Matt tells me as we're out for a walk. We've been talking about Griff and the texts and voice messages he continues to leave for me.

"It's over," I say, sounding a bit defensive. "It is so over. We. Are. Done."

"And so what are you going to do if he calls you?"

"He's not going to call. I'm telling you, Matt, it's over."

"Sure, Sally. He calls and says, 'Can we talk?' and you're going to shut him down? I don't think so."

I'm quiet for a moment, thinking about this. "Okay, so I'd probably talk to him. But he's not going to call. It's not an issue. This time it's *really* over."

But Matt knows what he's talking about. He's watched the relationship between Griff and me unfold over the past few years and he's already seen me through our first breakup. That time, Griff bolted, and I had absolutely no contact with him at all for a month.

I was angry, and quite determined to move on in my life. And then *Plenty of Fish* helpfully matched me up with a guy they thought would be perfect for me. It was Griff. It was so funny that I had to send him a message. He immediately phoned and asked me to meet him for dinner and the next thing I knew we were back together.

"This time is different," I tell Matt. "I am not going to put myself through this for a second time. I've learned my lesson."

By the time I get home that night, Griff has sent me one email and left two voice messages.

Which I return. Promptly.

All right then. Maybe we have a little bit of unfinished business.

And why can't I just accept that? Why can't I let this situation play out as it needs to? Why am I trying to convince myself that it is over and that I'm okay that it's over, when maybe I need a little more time?

The fact is that I really hate pain. I'll avoid it at all costs. I'm the girl who refuses to have even minor dental work without freezing.

My dentist knows this about me and arrives chairside with needle ready. I am devoted to him.

But I'm no better where emotional pain is concerned. I'll do anything to avoid it. And there's pain in this place. I've made it through the break up and now I just want to be able to move on. I want control. I want certainty. And I can get that by convincing myself that Griff and I are finished – and that I'm okay with it. It's a way to protect myself.

Except that it doesn't work. The minute I see Griff's name on my phone, the minute I hear his voice, or read a message from him, I'm thrown into the tumult of hope and despair.

And so I'm forced to take Matt's wise advice. I try to stop controlling the situation, and just let it play out. I'm working on staying open to the experience and to learning what I can about myself in this place, even if that means being vulnerable and risking more pain. And I'm working on finding my calm, still center, so that whatever happens, I will be okay.

One of the ways, I try to move forward is to look at things as honestly as I can. I think of my friend Elaine, who is an artist, and who recently ran a painting class for a small group of our girlfriends. "The most important thing you have to do when sketching," she cautioned, "is to see the object exactly as it is, not as you think it is." As we carefully sketched our pieces of fruit, she kept reminding us, "See things clearly.

It was good advice, and not just for hapless beginning artists like me, who hadn't any idea how to create a still life in acrylic. As I worked on my pear, I began to notice the way the light fell on it, the patches of shadow. I could see its blemishes and surprising contours. I could see the variations in its colour. Though my painting was clearly the work of a beginner, you could see the light and the shadow and the blemishes.

So that I can move on, I need to be sure to paint my relationship with Griff just as clearly and honestly. It's so easy for me to focus on only the good. I need to remember how anxious and insecure I was becoming and how clingy. If I'm going to move on, I need to remind myself that it was I who would not grant Griff full access to my life and especially my family. At some level I knew all along that he wasn't the right man for me.

It's funny how quickly life changes. For the last two years, I've paid virtually no attention to anything in the media about dating. Now, once again, I read and listen to everything with rapt attention.

Last week, my friend Helen handed me a newspaper clipping about mid-life dating. The most important tip? Dye your hair. This is significant as Helen has opted to grow older gracefully and has let her hair turn naturally grey. It looks beautiful on her. Recently, a second friend also opted to go grey. On her, the grey is handsome. But all along, I have been vehemently resistant to the idea.

Turns out, it was the right thing. Because, seriously, how could I be back out on the dating scene without dark, glossy locks. My hair stylist's livelihood is safe with women like me. Not only am I vain, but also, at some point I'd like to have sex again. With someone who is not 87.

Just before Valentine's Day, I listen to a CBC Radio special on online dating. A month ago, I wouldn't have paid any attention. Now that I'm single, however, I listen to every word, even taking a few notes throughout the program.

Here's the most interesting thing I learn: apparently the online dating market is now so enormous that it can support all kinds of niche sites. There are dating sites for seniors, for lesbians, and my particular favourite, a dating site for Jewish mothers who are looking for matches for their sons and daughters.

I am not making this up. There really is a site called *The J Moms*, a place where Jewish parents post profiles of themselves and make connections with other like-minded Jewish families. Once the Jewish mothers establish a relationship, they trade profiles of their offspring. Presumably the offspring are aware that this is all happening.

I'm trying to imagine a prospect more terrifying than having my mother involved in my dating life. I can't really think of anything.

So, since I'm not prepared to have my mother act as a matchmaker, I'll have to trust in my own abilities to find a suitable man. I've done it before. I'm pretty sure I can do it again. And I can take heart in knowing that the dating sites are devising ever more complicated algorithms to match me with the man of my dreams.

I can attest to the fact that these algorithms work. The first time Griff and I broke up, I signed up for *Plenty of Fish* and put together a new profile. It took the site exactly two days to find me my perfect match. I recognized the photo of Griff right away.

It was one I'd taken of him.

Of course, I was quite indignant to discover that he was already dating again. How dare he! He should have been at home drinking scotch and listening to "Ain't No Sunshine when She's Gone." And he definitely shouldn't have been using a picture I took of him!

Eventually I remembered that I was on the same site, probably using photos he took of me. After having refused to speak to him for more than a month, I contacted him and we ended up back together.

But that's not going to happen this time. I am not getting back together with Griff and I am not getting back on a dating website anytime soon. I'm hopeful, though, that when I'm ready, those algorithms will match me up with a man who I can love, a man who shares my interests and values; hopefully he'll also be taller than me and not a homicidal maniac.

I know I'm not ready for dating, because I am still not over Griff. I can be all sensible and rational and catalogue the many reasons he was *Not the Guy For Me*. But then he phones and leaves a voice message and I actually have a physical reaction just listening to his voice. My heart pounds; my hands shake; I am a hot mess.

He calls one day with news. He has finished the renovation and has walked the building inspector through the house for the last time. It's a huge relief for me: we have no further need to see or to speak to one another. I can move on.

But I still miss him and still feel really sad about our ending. I go back to my journal and read over all the reasons Griff and I can't stay together. But do you remember how the palm reader told me that my head and my heart do not communicate? It's clear that they're still not on speaking terms. I know that I need to let go of Griff, but I'm having a really hard time doing so.

A few days later, I find myself in my therapist's office again, trying to make sense of my situation. "I've been here before," I tell Linda. "I don't want to be here again. I've done enough of broken-hearted and single."

Linda gives me a sympathetic smile and waits for me to continue.

"I keep asking myself what I'm supposed to be learning here. It seems like the universe keeps having to send me the same lesson over and over."

"Any observations?" Linda asks.

"Mostly that I am a very slow learner." I try to laugh. Linda smiles, but doesn't respond. It's clear she's waiting for a serious answer.

"I'm learning about self worth," I start. "I never felt completely secure with Griff."

"What was that about?"

"I don't really know. I think of myself as being pretty strong and confident."

"But with Griff?"

I pause, not sure how to proceed. "I never fully trusted that Griff loved me for who I was. He had all these fancy watches and expensive clothes. He drove a luxury sports car." I falter. "I sometimes worried that I was just another shiny accessory in his life."

"Flattering, but not grounds for a solid relationship," Linda observes.

I nod. "I never felt as though the things I think are important about me – my intelligence, my creativity, the way I parent – I didn't feel like Griff valued those things. I think that left me feeling unbalanced."

"So in your next relationship, you want a man who recognizes your inner gifts."

"Someone who really gets me."

"What else are you learning?"

I pause to think a moment. "I've got some work to do around commitment."

Linda waits as I formulate my thoughts. "I know I want more from my next relationship. I want a full commitment. I want a guy who can be part of my whole life."

"You've been moving toward this understanding for a while I think."

I nod, remembering the sadness I used to feel every time I heard about another couple moving in or getting married. I knew that was never going to happen for me with Griff.

Linda nods. She's heard me talk about this before.

"But at the same time, the whole idea of meeting somebody and moving in together terrifies me."

"What scares you?"

I take a deep breath, trying not to cry. "I don't want to screw up my kids. That more than anything."

"Sally, you've worked hard to give your boys a calm, stable home life. That's not going to change."

I feel myself starting to cry and to laugh all at once. "I don't actually know why I'm even worrying about any of this. The reality is that where my kids are concerned, I'm completely inflexible. I'm not prepared to move. I'm not prepared to parent any differently.  I'm not prepared to do anything that would cause my guys any more upheaval. How am I ever going to find someone when I'm so set in my ways?"

"There's a difference between being inflexible and having clear boundaries."

"Sure. But I think I could try to be a bit more flexible."

"You don't have to give up what's most important to you in order to have a relationship. You don't have to compromise."

I give Linda a weak smile, but I'm skeptical.

"This isn't an either-or proposition, Sally. You can invite a loving, long-term partner into your life and still have a stable, happy family life. It is possible."

I let this sink in, trying to believe her. But I can't.

"Now," she says, "what are you doing to look after yourself right now? You've lost a lot of weight since I saw you last."

"At least 10 pounds," I admit. " I'm not sleeping. My hair is starting to fall out. I'm having a pretty hard time getting over this."

"Self care," Linda says sternly. "This should be your first priority."

And so following Linda's advice, I focus on long walks, bubble baths and B vitamins. I schedule things like dancing and photography back into my life. I make tentative plans for spring break and the summer, fun little adventures with my boys, things to look forward to. And I write my heart out, trying to learn the lessons I'm meant to learn in this place. Lessons like patience, for example.

In our twenties, my ex-husband and I climbed Mount Kilimanjaro. Before the climb, we stayed a couple of nights at the Marangu Hotel, a faded resort at the base of the mountain. And while there, we met the owner, Miss Erica Laani. Miss Erika was a tiny woman, who must have been in her eighties at that time, and who had climbed the mountain five times, the first time as a child.

As we set out on the first morning of the climb, Miss Erika, cautioned, "You must take it *pole pole*," Swahili for slowly, slowly.

It was good advice. "Kili" is not a technical climb, but it's over 19,000 feet high. We needed to move slowly in order to adjust to the altitude. For three days, we moved at a leisurely pace, stopping frequently to rest and admire the scenery. Even still, we felt the effects of the altitude. By the morning of the fourth day, and the ascent to the summit, I felt as though I had the flu; I was queasy, weak, and very tired. But all that stopping and resting and plodding along paid off: I'll never forget watching the sun rise above the clouds.

*Pole pole*. Over the years, I've often needed to remind myself of that important lesson. I am an impatient woman. And impulsive. My natural inclination is to rush through life. Particularly the unpleasant parts.

Like now, for instance. I am so ready to move on, to stop feeling sad, to find somebody new. I want to put this time behind me and march headlong into my next adventure. Where is the next love of my life? Surely, he must be just around the next corner!

And so, because I am not only impatient, but also an eternal optimist, I begin calling this next man into my life. I'm not ready for him to arrive just yet. I'm not ready for a new relationship, and I'm not even ready to create a profile and get myself out there on *Plenty of Fish*. I'm just ready for a gentle whisper: "Hey, universe? It isn't time yet, but keep your eyes open for me, okay?"

The universe has delivered often enough in the past that I trust in it. I know that once I am ready and once I am clear about the kind of man I want to find, the universe will send him my way. That's how Griff arrived. And Andrew before him. It's even how I got my job. And so, trusting in the universe, I begin thinking about the qualities I want my "One Good Man" to possess.

"I think I need to date a slacker surfer dude for a while," I joke with Kira. "I've kind of had it with the driven, Type A men who populate my past."

"Careful what you wish for," she cautions. Kira knows how the universe works too. And she's right, so I start taking this task a little more seriously, writing about what I want. I begin by generating a long list, a list that is really specific. I challenge myself to come up with a hundred ideas, any quality or detail that I would like my "One Good Man" to have. I'd like you to know that coming up with a hundred different ideas isn't easy and by the end, I have some interesting details on that list, details like, "he is a morning person and he reads Rohinton Mistry."

And this is why I need to narrow things down, not only because it might be unreasonable to ask so much from the universe, but also because I need to know which things are really important. I'm fairly confident that if the right guy turns out to be a night owl, it would not be a deal breaker for me. But the important thing is that I need a dating guide.

Remember how I told you that I could convince myself that dating the next contestant in the Iditarod could be a good idea? I know that once I start dating again, I will easily be blown off course.

"Okay," I tell Kira. "Number One. There has to be chemistry."

"Amen, Sister!"

"I've had good chemistry. I'm never going back."

"Nope. Totally with you on that."

"Number two, he has to have a kind heart. I want a man who is warm and affectionate."

Kira nods, though she doesn't seem as enthusiastic about my second point.

"Also, thoughtful and considerate, someone who won't take advantage of my good nature, who won't always put his needs first."

"Important," Kira confirms.

"And light-hearted. I've done enough intense and brooding for one lifetime."

She laughs. "Yes, you have."

"No drama."

"Check."

"And he has to have an open mind. I can't do rigid, black and white thinking. It doesn't work at all for me."

"Yep. That was a problem for you with Griff."

I nod. "Intelligent. And adventurous. I want to find someone who likes the idea of wandering through a night market somewhere in Asia, someone who doesn't need first class accommodation."

Kira smiles. She's known me long enough to understand my need for adventure.

"And this last one? Scares the hell out of me, but it's important. I want someone who is ready for a long-term, full commitment."

Silence from Kira. She's shaking her head. "I don't know about that one. There's something to be said for all fun and no commitment."

I laugh. "I know. Been there. But I'm ready for more now. I don't want to spend another three years dating someone who lives across town, knowing the relationship is going nowhere."

"Okay, this sounds like a good list," Kira says, "but you've left out the most important thing." I wait for her to explain, expecting "Rich" or "Hot" or "Amazing in bed."

Her response? "Must have a vasectomy."

Kira has always been so wise.

Though I'm ready for making and even sharing lists, I am not ready for dating. Just the thought of getting back onto a dating site makes me feel queasy. Instead, I follow Linda's advice and do everything I can to look after myself and to find myself again. I know that this is critical for me and that I will not find a new love until I've remembered fully how to love myself and love my life. It's another one of those lessons I keep having to learn.

And if I were a sensible woman, I would have just kept on with that plan for at least a few more months. But I don't think anyone has ever said to me, "Sally, thank you for being the sensible one here."

# THREE

## A IS FOR ADAM

It's because measured and rational are not among my virtues that I find myself out on my first date in nearly three years. Kira has orchestrated the date.

"Say no if you want to," she says one day while we're out for coffee. "But my friend Adam called me last night. Remember the guy with the coffee shops?"

One of Kira's many talents – besides juggling men – is that she effortlessly converts many of her first dates into friends. Adam is one of those friends and she tells me about him. He's a single dad, a guy who really seems to want to find somebody to share his life with. And it's a pretty good life. He made a good deal of money in the oil patch and then moved here and invested it. These days he runs a couple of lucrative franchises and has lots of time and money to play.

"He's so fed up with the dating scene and really wants to find a long-term partner. He phoned me today to see if I had any friends who might be looking for a nice guy..."

I wait for her to go on. "That list you made? I think he'd meet quite a few of your requirements. He's funny, smart, and successful. And," she says with a mischievous look on her face, "he's had a vasectomy." She waits until I stop laughing. "I checked. Just for you!"

In that moment I feel hope and anxiety rising in me all at once. (About the man. Not the vasectomy).

"It's kind of a coincidence, don't you think?" Kira asks.

I half shrug and half nod. My anxiety is mutating into terror.

"He's a good guy, just not for me. If you like, I could put you guys in touch."

I do my shrug-nod thing again. "Okay..."

"I mean, what have you got to lose?" Kira smiles at me. "It's just coffee. You don't have to marry the guy."

And so I find myself out for my first date in three years, having coffee with a guy that I've been jokingly referring to as a "Kira Castoff."

Even before we meet, just chatting on the phone, I find myself drawn to him. He is warm and funny and approachable. "You have no idea how much I want to meet you," he tells me. "I so want to prove my girls wrong." By his girls, he means a group of his employees who have helped him launch an online dating profile;

they are confident that this is where he'll meet the woman of his dreams.

I point out that technically we *are* meeting because of the Internet: that's how he met Kira, and if it weren't for Kira, we wouldn't have met. "True," he concedes. "But if it works out, you have to promise never to reveal the online dating connection. It's just so humiliating!" I laugh with him, remembering how awkward it used to feel when people would ask how I met Griff.

I arrive a few minutes early to the coffee shop, feeling sick with anxiety. It's pouring with rain outside and I've made a breathless sprint for shelter, mostly to preserve my hair, which I've painstakingly straightened. The clothes will dry. The make-up can be retouched. But the hair? Once it's wet, all hope is lost. Really, I should have waited until May to start dating again.

I've spent hours agonizing over what to wear for this half-hour coffee date. I've decided on polished and professional, given that I'm meeting Adam after work, and so I'm wearing a cute blouse, a pencil skirt, and high-heeled boots. The plan is to look good in an effortless sort of way. Adam does not need to know about the agonizing. Nor does he need to know on this first date how truly vain I really am. I'm running my fingers through my still-dry locks when Adam walks in.

In person, he's good looking, with a great smile, and a rugged build. He is not a tall man, but he has the most impressive set of biceps I've encountered in a while. He displays these biceps when he pulls up his sleeve to show me the tattoos on his arms: a Canadian flag, a set of stylized Hawaiian turtles, and a '66 Mustang, just like the one in his garage. His arms are beautiful: in fact, he might be worth a second date just for his body. He's funny too, and wealthy and adventurous. Really, what's not to like?

I'm a little uncomfortable when he places his Porsche key fob on the table between us. It's clear he wants me to notice it, to ask him about his car. I don't. And then throughout the conversation, he drops multiple references to his wealth, describing his frequent holidays to Hawaii, Mexico and the Caribbean, places he escapes to when the island starts to feel too small for him. He even tells me how much he paid for the franchises he operates. He is under the impression that money is the way to a woman's heart. And though I joke about being a trophy wife, the truth is that money just isn't that important to me. Griff had lots of money and at first I loved the way he showered me with gifts and drove me around in his expensive little convertible. But eventually, his preoccupation with accumulating more wealth became a source of tension between us.

Adam, of course, is unaware of this, and rattles on nervously, telling me about his expensive hobbies and many investments.

"So, yeah, that's it, really. That's me in a nutshell." He looks uncomfortable. He's fidgeting and having trouble keeping eye contact. I don't know if it's something about me that's making him anxious or whether it's just the whole first coffee date thing he's struggling with. On paper, he's a man with everything going for him. I'm not sure why he isn't more relaxed and confident.

And I wonder how I'm coming across to him. I'm nervous too and seriously out of dating practice. I've forgotten how prepared I need to be, how ready I need to be to pick up the conversation. But even as I'm processing all this, I'm focussing on one key thing: he is not for me.

I know this with absolute certainty, and within fifteen minutes of meeting him. But I'm not disappointed. I'm relieved. It is so good to know that I haven't lost my judgment, that I can trust my instincts, and trust I'm not going to end up in a relationship unless it's just right.

And so in early March, I find myself penning my first *Thanks but no thanks* email:

*Hi Adam,*

*Thank you so much for coffee today. I enjoyed your sense of humour and appreciated your honesty. And – I have to say – those are impressive biceps. Honestly, I'm surprised you're still single. But I don't think it's going to work out for us. I'm an island girl, and I need someone who wants to be here, who isn't trying to escape this place.*

*I wish you well, Adam.*

*Sally*

As I write the note, I feel like I'm making a really healthy decision. My date with Adam highlighted many of the problems that existed in my relationship with Griff, reminding me not to romanticize things now that it's over. Also it showed me pretty clearly that I shouldn't be dating yet. I know from this first meeting that I am not ready. I tell myself that for a while longer, I should forego men all together, and not even think about dating. I tell myself that I should just be taking care of myself.

Like any sensible woman would.

But that whole sensible, measured, patient thing is just so hard for me.

Which is how I end up, kind of by accident, signing onto a dating website less than a week later. I don't mean to. I am under the impression that I can fill out the personality profile, find out some cool information about myself, and then wait a while before actually signing up.

Apparently that's not how this website works.

The minute I hit "submit" on the personality quiz, the site starts generating matches for me. Within minutes, nine men can see my incomplete profile. This, of course, sends me into a complete panic. First of all, I have no intention of signing up just yet. I am not ready!

And second, I don't have any fabulous profile pictures to post.

Can you tell I'm a Pisces?

Here I am, once again, swimming off in opposite directions. The wise Sally would have refrained from taking the personality quiz simply because it was connected to a dating site. The wise Sally wouldn't have been anywhere near a dating site. The wise Sally would have spent the evening writing in her journal, soaking in a bubble bath and reflecting on her growth.

The impulsive Sally, however, has different plans.

After I stop panicking, I realize that there is an easy solution: I'll just hide my profile until I'm ready to date again. I spend an hour poking around on the site before I come to the horrifying conclusion that I cannot hide here. And worse, I am starting to get messages.

Another hour and I know I need back up.

"Kira, I need your help." The minute she answers the phone, I start talking.

"I accidentally signed up for *eHarmony* tonight and I don't know how anything works. It is *way* different than *Plenty of Fish!*"

"Accidentally?" she laughs.

"It's a long story. But you need to explain to me how to hide my profile."

"On *eHarmony*? That, my friend, is a nearly impossible task."

I groan. “Can you at least explain this place to me? What am I supposed to do after someone sends me questions? I answered them, but it looks like he's sent more and I don't know how to access them."

"No, no, no," she says. "After you answer his questions, you're supposed to send *him* some questions. And, really, most people do that right away."

"Oh no! I answered his questions an hour ago. I didn't send him any back. Maybe I should send him a message and apologize."

"No! You'd have to request personal communication and you don't want to do that too soon."

"This is so complicated! And what am I supposed to do with the 'icebreakers'? I don't understand what any of these things mean. Someone sent me one. And Kira, you should see him. I mean, he might be a lovely guy, but I have to be honest, I can't imagine ever dating somebody so unkempt. You should see his hair. I can't even describe how bad his hair is. It’s just the very worst comb-over you’ve ever seen."

"Yeah," Kira sighed, the weight of her dating years in her voice. "You know, the thing about a lot of men is that they just don't get the concept of 'League.'

“I’m not following...”

“You know. League.  As in you and I are *so not* in the same league."

“Ha! You should see that hair. It’s unbelievable.”

“Oh, honey. You don’t know what I’ve seen.”

"I know. I'm sorry. And I need your help! What am I supposed to with these guys? I don't want to be mean. I sent 'Bad Hair Man' a smile. You know, polite. Not interested, thanks."

"Oh no! This is not good! Sally, a smile is like a wink. It says 'I like the look of you.' Do not send any more smiles!"

"I am so bad at this!

"You'll figure it out," Kira laughs.

"And here's one more question. Are these guys all using their real names? It's so different than *Plenty of Fish* that way. It was always a laugh getting messages from The Chick Whisperer and Sexy Cougar Hunter. It's not as much fun to get a message from Bob."

"Yeah. It's different. Most people use their own names."

"Did you, when you started?"

"Uh. No." Kira sounds a little uncomfortable.

"So what kind of a name did you use?" I am so bummed already that I can't be Serendipity or Delicious.

Kira pauses before she answers me. "I don't really know how to tell you this. When I first signed up, I was Sally."

Now it's my turn to pause. "What?"

"Yeah. Sorry. I didn't want to use my own name and I kind of wanted to channel your good dating energy."

I'm laughing by now. "So what you're telling me is that I will be the second Sally from our little town to show up on this site in two years! What a coincidence!"

Kira is laughing too. "On the bright side, I'll be able to screen all your dates."

"What do you mean?"

"Well, we're two professional women in our forties. We both live out this way and have kids. We're both petite brunettes. Chances are that you will get paired up with some of the same guys I dated when I was there."

"I'm trying to see how that is good."

"There were some good guys. Just not right for me. You know what they say about one man's junk."

"No! Stop!" We're both in hysterics.

"Listen," Kira says. "My advice is just to keep a really low profile. Stay off the website. Don't respond to anyone just yet. Unless they're really cute of course."

# FOUR

# B IS FOR BEN

Taking Kira's advice to heart, I spend the next few weeks staying as far away from the dating website as I can. I hadn't filled out my profile during the inadvertent sign up, so only a few men contacted me when my nearly blank profile first appeared, and then things fell quiet. I'd been worried about how to refrain from engaging, because I'd always believed that anyone who put himself out there enough to make contact with me at least deserved a response. But I didn't really hear much from anyone.

Instead I throw myself into the pursuits I love. When my boys are home, I spend as much time as I can with them, and once they're in bed, I write. When the kids are with their dad, I arrange coffee, drinks or long hikes with friends. When I met Griff I had been so consumed with my own interests and plans that I had little time to fit him into my life. I was in a very healthy space, truly nourishing myself and moving forward in my life.

Healthy, I think. That's the place I need to get back to. Before I date, I need to be that healthy again.

So sane. So sensible. So rational. And then Ben contacts me.

I awake one morning to a new *eHarmony* notification. I'm a bit cranky about even going to the website, because the handful of men who have so far contacted me seem so completely unsuitable that I can't believe people actually pay money to become full members. Why am I being contacted by men so much older than me? By men who live so far away? By men with such bad hair?

I click on the new message to see a wink from someone called Ben. I sigh dramatically; another guy, just randomly sending winks out across the dating site, hoping that *someone* might respond, I think. A few weeks and I'm already cynical.

But as Ben's profile comes up on my screen, my cynicism turns to surprise. A rangy-looking, athletic man smiles out at me; this guy is seriously good looking. Interested, I scroll through his other photos: in a second photo, he is passing a ball on a rugby pitch; in a third, he stands flanked by two other men, their arms draped around each other's shoulders. The three look like brothers. My surprise turns to curiosity.

I read through his brief profile: professional; engaged in his community; the father of a little girl, younger than my three boys; athletic; and did I mention cute?

His profile indicates he is looking for a long-term commitment. I could do long term with this guy!

I wink back.

When I return home from work that evening, I immediately check my home email. Nothing. I feel disappointment wash over me. For the first time, I've seen somebody who looks promising and he hasn't responded.

The next morning, there is another notification, more communication from Ben, this time a set of random-seeming questions, to which I can only choose from multiple choice answers. Frustrated, I text Kira. *What is with men on this site? Why don't they just send me a message?*

She texts me back right away. *It's not the men. It's the site. You have to do what's called Guided Communication. Questions first. Then messages.*

Before I finish reading the first text, a second one arrives: *I thought you were staying away from there!*

*Got a wink and questions from a very cute guy*, I text back.

*Name? Details? I might have dated him.*

*Ben. Tall, cute, single dad, rugby player. Sound familiar?*

*Nope. Let me know what happens!!*

I answer Ben's multiple-choice questions and choose some to send back to him, feeling hope rising once more. But when I get home, nothing. Disappointment again. I've completely forgotten what a roller coaster online dating can be.

Just before I head off to bed, there is another notification: a request for private communication. Cursing this dating site designed for prudent and patient people, I click yes and go off to brush my teeth. And then – I can't help myself – I check my email one more time before bed. And there is an actual message from Ben.

It's a lovely, chatty email, apologizing for his late-night responses the last couple of nights. He's been at a conference, he explains. Expressing relief to be able to finally communicate in writing, he asks me a couple of questions about myself, tells me he hopes to hear from me soon, and wishes me sweet dreams.

I can't sleep now! I immediately respond, thanking him for his email, answering his questions, and asking a few of my own. I hit "send," with full intentions of heading off to bed. But within a few minutes he sends me a new message, and I realize that I am probably going to have a late night.

Over the next few evenings, I rush my two younger boys through their bedtime routines and spend a bit of time with my fifteen-year-old. But as soon as he tires of my company, I head off to connect with Ben. For the first couple of days, I check for messages and we spend the evening chatting online, but soon, Ben suggests a phone call.

Panic rises. I've always been better in person than on the phone. I find it far more difficult to get to a place that feels comfortable on the phone. But as soon as I hear Ben say my name, as soon as I hear his hearty laugh and his lovely English accent, I feel completely at ease. He is easy and comfortable and relaxed and our conversation is light hearted and wide-ranging. I can hardly wait to meet him.

We want to meet. But the boys are with me for more than a week, and Ben has his daughter for a few days on and a few days off at a time. I realize with surprise that in all the time I have dated, I have never chosen to go out with a man who has actual, hands-on parenting responsibilities. I've dated dads with adult children and dads who have financial responsibilities for their children but who have chosen to live away from their kids. What does it say about me, I muse, that I have probably dated twenty-five men since my divorce and among them, not one was actually raising a child?

When I met Griff, I wanted fun and no strings. I didn't want anyone who might have potentially threatened my safe little family dynamic, a dynamic that was working very nicely. I was good at being a single mom. My kids were happy and well adjusted and there was no way I was going to let somebody into the inner circle of my family if he had chosen not to have kids at all or if he had chosen to take only financial responsibility as a parent. Those twenty-five men without parenting responsibilities were safe choices! They were looking for fun and so was I.

But now here was Ben, talking fondly about his daughter's days and my heart was melting. It was so clear that I was meant to be with somebody who valued family as much as I did.

Finally, after nearly a week, we are able to meet on a Saturday morning.

I arrive a few minutes late, churned up with anxiety and second-guessing today's outfit. I have to say that "coffee and a walk" dates present a huge challenge for a woman like me. I have a closet full of cute clothes and shoes, but most of them are not suitable for a circuit around one of the local lakes or along a waterfront pathway. Do I wear yoga gear and running shoes? Sensible but hardly enticing. It's too early in the season for capris and sandals and a bit late for leggings and boots. What if the trail is muddy?

So much for effortless style.

I recognize Ben as soon as I enter the coffee shop, lanky and dressed in jeans and a light down jacket. He stands to greet me, smiling.

"I'm so sorry I'm late," I start, but he laughs, his blue eyes crinkling and his smile wide.

"Don't worry about it," he says, hugging me warmly. "It's nice to finally meet you." His accent is even better in person. We pull away from the hug, but stand looking at each other for a moment, both of us smiling. *Uh oh*, I think. *This man might be trouble.*

Ben gestures for me to sit, asks what I'd like to drink, and heads off to order my coffee. As he waits, he keeps looking back at me, a big grin still on his face. I can't help but smile back, delighted that he doesn't feel any need to play it cool. When he returns to our table, he places the coffee in front of me, and then gives my shoulder a squeeze before he sits down. "You're just as pretty in person as you are in your pictures," he says, and leans toward me with a smile.

Our first date lasts three hours, extending into lunch, and during that time we talk non-stop, sharing stories and finding a number of connections. It's probably the most promising first date I've ever been on.

*Dear Ben,*

*I told you about my plan to blog about my dating adventures. I figured I'd get to at least S is for Stefan before I'd meet somebody with potential. But as our quick coffee date turned into a three hour lunch, I realized that maybe it was going to take a little longer to get to S is for Stefan than I first anticipated. I would love to meet you next Saturday for dinner.*

*Until then I remain,*

*S is for Sally*

"Just take your time," my counsellor reminds me. I'm sitting in her office and I am beyond agitated. That coffee date with Ben has morphed into a relationship that within a matter of weeks is accelerating at warp speed. We've been out together a number of times and have been spending late nights on Skype. The saving grace has been that we can't see one another very often because of our respective – and nearly opposite – parenting schedules.

"Remember," my counsellor cautions, "you have to give a new relationship lots of time to develop. Don't move from the front porch too soon."

The front porch. It's an apt metaphor, that place in a relationship where we slowly get to know one another, where we share tea and polite, easy conversation, where the focus is on friendship and companionship. The front porch. It's a good reminder, particularly for an impulsive woman like me, so quick to embrace the next thing, so happy to say yes to opportunity and possibility. It's even more important with a man like Ben. If I am the kind of person who says yes to life, Ben is a man who says, "Hell, Yes!"

We are a dangerous combination.

But just as things start to feel like they might become serious, Griff strolls back into my life, arriving unannounced one afternoon. When I open the door and see him standing there, hands in pockets, a half smile playing across his face, I can't catch my breath. He's dressed in jacket and tie, and looks like he just walked out of a GQ magazine. "I have some paperwork for you," he says, his voice as warm as a long hug. I stand mute for a long minute before opening the door wide and inviting him in.

"Would you like tea?" I ask, my voice weak.

"Please."

We sit down together at the kitchen table, and before I can say anything, he puts his hand on top of mine and squeezes it. I look up at him and the minute our eyes meet, we're drawn together. Magnet and steel is not a strong enough metaphor.

Once Griff leaves, I email Ben, making an excuse for why I can't Skype with him that night. I know that I wouldn't be able to hide my confusion. I need time to make sense of the afternoon. Instead of talking to Ben, I phone Kira instead and tell her the whole story.

"Oh, honey," she says, clucking sympathetically. "Maybe it really isn't over between you and Griff."

"Oh, it's over," I say miserably. "We can't keep our hands off one another, but it's definitely over." I think of Griff's hand on my cheek, how he stroked my face sadly before he left, as though committing it to memory.

"Why didn't he just drop off the paperwork when he knew you wouldn't be home?"

"I don't know," I say. "And why didn't I just take it and send him on his way?"

There's a long pause at the other end of the line. "Do you think he could be reading your blog? Do you think he read about Ben?"

The thought hasn't crossed my mind.

Later that night, I send Griff a quick email and suggest that it would be better if we didn't see each other again. Then I send Ben an email. I don't tell him about my encounter with Griff, but I do tell him about my conversation about the front porch, and suggest that we slow things down a little. Even before Griff appeared, I was struggling. Now I'm even more disoriented.

The front porch. I see how important this place is for Ben and me. Things have moved too fast between us, and now I'm also grappling with my longing for and guilt about Griff. Ben agrees to pull back a bit, and we limit ourselves for the next couple of weeks to emails and the occasional Skype call. But inevitably, we begin Skyping and texting more and find ourselves again talking long into every evening and trying to find times when we're both free to meet.

I really like Ben. When we're together, our conversation is easy and laced with laughter. He's an affectionate man, and I love that he pulls me close to him when we walk and holds my hand over dinner. I like his humour and his relaxed approach to life and his easy devotion to his daughter. I enjoy our conversations and I find him attractive. But there is something holding me back.

I suspect it is pure terror.

"I want to move forward with you," he tells me. So open. So courageous. "I am ten toes in," he says.

But the more serious he gets, the faster I back away. I start to feel annoyed that he wants to talk to me every single night. I'm irritated that he taps his feet, that he clears his throat, that he tells the same stories time and again. They're small things, inconsequential, but I can't help focusing on them. I make lists of all the things I like about Ben and all the things I'm worried about. I spend hours reading articles on the Internet with titles like, "Ten Ways to Know If He is the One." I agonize. I lose sleep.

I'm sure that in part, it's because my relationship with Griff ended so recently. But it's something else too, something much bigger. Ben is the first man since my divorce who is really looking for a long-term relationship. He's done his work. He's ready. And he sees me as a woman he could happily grow old with.

Isn't this exactly what I wanted?

Apparently not.

*Hi Ben,*

*I got off our Skype call last night and cried. There is so much about you that I find attractive. You embody so many of the qualities I'm looking for in a man. And I have so much fun hanging out with you. But it's all moving way too fast for me. I wish I were in a place where I could offer you as much as you seem ready to offer me. But I can't. I am just not ready.*

*Thank you for understanding that I need time and space to breathe. I hope that there is someone waiting for you just around the next corner, Ben.*

*Sally*

The moment I end things with Ben, my anxiety lifts. I can breathe deeply again. I can spend my evenings writing or reading, instead of talking on Skype. I can stop worrying about whether I'm making the right choice.

"He was too into me, too enthusiastic," I tell Linda. "It just didn't feel right."

"Perhaps," my therapist suggests, "he can see in you what you can't yet see yourself."

That silences me.

About a week after I end things with Ben, just about the time the anxiety finally dissipates, I wake one morning thinking I've made a huge mistake. Without the sense of panic, I can see again what a good man Ben is. Impulsively I send him an email, apologizing for ending things and asking him if he'd consider getting back together with me.

His reply is diplomatic and very clear.

*Sally,*

*There is so much that is beautiful about you. There's a part of me that wants to give you another chance. But I know that you aren't ready for a relationship. I hope that when you are ready, a good man will come along for you. There are a few of us out there. What I really hope is that with me you've at least had a peek over the fence, a glimpse of what commitment looks like.*

*Ben*

"You are such an idiot," Matt tells me. We're out walking and I've just confessed the whole, messy Ben story. "What the hell are you doing on a site like *eHarmony* right now? The only people who are on that site are looking for serious and long term."

"Well," I start, trying to contain my indignation. "First of all I didn't mean to end up on that site." I pause so Matt can complete his dramatic eye rolling routine. "And second, I don't want to spend another year on *Plenty of Fish* dating another twenty-five men, none of whom is really suitable for me."

"Look, I'm telling you, you are in the wrong place. I've been on *eHarmony* and the people there are serious about happily ever after."

"I'm serious about happily ever after!" I protest. "But maybe not just yet."

"I think you should try out *Match,*" Matt decides. "It's kind of in between. You won't get the anything-goes, free-for-all craziness of *Plenty of Fish*. But there will be people on the site like you, ready for some fun, but not necessarily ready to commit right now." He looks at me speculatively. "And I think I should help you with your profile."

Which is how I end up at Matt's place doing an impromptu analysis of my competition. He's done a search and brought up all the women in Victoria within a five-year age range of me. I'm surprised there aren't more of us.

Matt starts scrolling through the profiles. "Nope. Nope. Nope." He's dismissing a number of them just based on the photos.

"We should look at some of them," I suggest.

"No, hang on." He scrolls through a few more, and then clicks on the profile of a pretty blond woman. "This is what you're aiming for," he says, obviously familiar with this particular profile. The photos show an attractive woman engaged in a variety of outdoor pursuits, hiking, walking a beach, standing beside a kayak.

"She looks so good in all her photos. I never look that good."

"We'll take some new ones of you, down at the beach or something."

I laugh. "Like a profile photo shoot?"

Matt nods at the profile that's open on his screen. "You don't really think that those are all candids, do you?"

My eyes widen. "You think those are staged?"

He shrugs. "I wouldn't be surprised." He returns to the search, bringing up a badly lit selfie of a woman leering into the camera. She's wearing a dog collar and a low cut top. "This is what you don't want."

"No shit! Do you actually think I'd post something like that?"

"No, but it's a good reminder about the difference between hot and not."

Matt returns to the search option, typing in a username. He's clearly familiar with a number of the women on the site. "Check out this woman's written profile," he says. "I'm half in love with her just reading it." He gives me time to read her sweet and quirky introduction.

"Her personality comes through so clearly, hey?" I say.

"Yeah. And look at that adorable picture of her in that floppy hat."

It is adorable.

But someone has to say it.

"Matt, she's twenty-four. That's, like, twenty-four years younger than you."

Matt gives me a rueful smile. His last girlfriend wasn't yet thirty and he has a long string of much younger women in his dating history.

"You should actually try dating someone your own age."

"I have! They just feel so...old."

"Thanks," I say, laughing, and well aware of the fact that I'm only a couple of years younger than him. It's an ongoing discussion between us. How young is too young? How old is too old? The kinds of philosophical questions I never thought I'd be having in my mid-forties. And the kind of questions that are front of mind as I start working on a new profile for *Match*.

After some back and forth with Matt over the photos and the write-up, I'm ready to launch a new profile. I have a small selection of photos, carefully curated by Matt. He's forbidden me to include one of my favourites, a picture of me in profile on the back of a sailboat in Greece.

"Look how weird your chin looks," Matt says.

"I don't think it looks weird!" But as I examine it closely, I see what he means. "Look how great my shoulders look, though!" I'm quite pleased with my shoulders in this shot. They're toned and, after a couple of weeks on the Aegean, deeply bronzed. I still think I should keep the photo.

"Nobody actually cares about your shoulders," Matt points out. "And I'm giving you the guy's perspective here. Your chin looks all pointy. Ditch that photo."

The picture is dropped. Instead, there's a picture of me dressed up, holding a glass of champagne. "Yeah, you look elegant. Classy," Matt decides. There's a picture of me on a winter beach. "Good. Outdoorsy. Nice." And I've chosen a different picture of me on the sailboat, smiling into the camera. I don't like it as much because my shoulders are definitely better than my legs, but Matt likes it. "That's a nice smile. Open. Kind of inviting. And you're looking all adventurous on that boat."

I choose a username – Serendipity - and load my profile with the tag line, "Heading in New Directions." And then I compose my first profile in a few years. I'm mindful about who I might be calling into my life. One good man, I think, as I read over my writing one last time.

*Sometimes I look at myself and wonder, "How on earth did I end up here?" Don't get me wrong: "here" is a pretty great place to be. I certainly have no regrets. Over the years, I've had some amazing adventures, exploring the beauty of B.C. and of the world beyond. I've hiked and kayaked, backpacked, sailed, and camped. (I've stayed in a few nice hotels along the way, too. The truth is that my closet contains more heels than hiking boots.) Over the last five years, I've also been on a pretty intensive journey of self-growth; it's a journey that continues.*

*I think sometimes about the books I could write. They'd have titles like "The Delicious Life: A Woman's Guide to Being Single" or "Contained Chaos: On Raising Boys."*

*I'm excited about what lies ahead on the journey. I don't know exactly where I'm going, but I know there will be time along the way for travel and outdoor adventure, time for family and friends, time for more learning, and time for building a deep and enduring relationship.*

*I'm drawn to men who are positive and playful, who are adventurous, intelligent and warm. I like laughter, curiosity and good conversation. I value open communication, commitment to growth, honesty and loyalty. And I love to be touched.*

I hit submit and then I settle in, waiting to see what might happen next.

# FIVE

## C IS FOR CHRIS

"I am so bad at saying no," I tell Matt after my first *Match* date. He and I are out for a photo shoot, looking for a few good, up-to-date pictures to add to my profile. *Match*, it seems, is a more profitable venue for a girl like me. Where *eHarmony* controls who can see me and when, *Match* allows its users to see everyone. And so, after I figure out how to adjust my settings to prevent messages from men in Utah and Oman, I settle into a nice, comfortable rhythm, communicating with a few local men, men like Chris.

Chris contacted me as soon as I joined the site. A pilot, world traveler, and a person deeply engaged in a journey of self-discovery, Chris sent me a series of well-written and thoughtful messages, and when he invited me to meet him for dinner one night in a local pub, I was happy to accept. The evening did not go exactly as planned.

I tell Matt about the meeting. "First of all, he was a good ten years older than his profile stated. I don't get why anyone would lie about his age! Do they think we won't notice it when we meet them in person?" I'd had to contain my surprise when Chris met me outside a local pub. He must have been using profile photographs that were pretty dated, and though he was still an attractive man, he couldn't have been a day under sixty.

Matt shakes his head sympathetically. "That hasn't really happened too much to me," he says. "But, yeah, I think it's pretty common." We are at the beach and he's looking for a good place to take some photos of me.

"And, you know, age isn't a deal breaker for me. If I met someone who I really connected with who was, say, ten years older, I'd consider him. The question is why anyone in his sixties would want to date a woman with an 8 year old?"

Matt just laughs and shrugs. "Kids aren't necessarily a deal breaker. Maybe Pilot Boy misses the days when his kids were little."

"Pilot Boy has never married and never had kids." I stop and think about this for a moment. "And you know, one of these days I'm going to stop dating guys like that!" I pause again and laugh. "Guys like you!"

"It's definitely a pattern for you." Matt grins and then points to a rocky outcrop. "Let's take some pictures up there."

"And here's the other thing," I add, clambering over the rocks. "All the way through dinner, he kept touching me. You know, putting his hand on my hand, rubbing my knee. It was really creepy."

Matt is laughing loudly now. "And at the end of the date he kissed me. On the mouth! With tongue!" I stop and look at Matt, who is still laughing. "This is not funny!"

"You're the one who put something in her profile about how you love to be touched."

"Yeah, but not on a first date!"

"Well, you should probably say that on your profile."

"What. Like a disclaimer?"

"Yeah. The Fine Print."

Now we're both laughing. Matt removes the lens cap and starts shooting photos. "Stand over there. A little bit taller."

"So how do you graciously say no?" I ask, as Matt snaps more photos.

"Turn this way a bit. Smile!" He clicks a few more pictures and then puts the camera down. "The best way to say no is to make the other person feel like it's their idea," he tells me. "You could say, 'thanks for getting together the other night' and all that, and then add, 'I can see we are in different places in our lives and that you are probably looking for somebody who has more free time than I do.' Then leave it in their ballpark."

I think about this a bit. "I'm going to try that," I say. "You are a dating genius!"

I find a tidal pool and crouch down to inspect it. Matt picks up the camera again and circles around me. "Oh yeah! These are going to be good! Lean forward a little more. Nice!" I notice he's zooming in on my chest.

"What are you doing?"

"These are profile pictures. Remember?"

Right. I lean forward and give him my sunniest smile.

*Dear Chris,*

*It was lovely to finally meet you. I enjoyed our conversation, and found your stories about your recent trip to the Andes fascinating. It sounds like the experience was intensely spiritual for you.*

*I enjoyed hearing about your experiences as a pilot too. Your joy of "slipping the surly bonds of earth" is infectious.*

*Though I really enjoyed meeting you, I can see that we are in different places in our lives. With a full-time job and three kids, I just don't have very much time. I think you're looking for a woman with more availability in her life.*

*I wish you all the best in your search, Chris.*

*Sally*

# SIX

# D IS FOR DAN

So Victoria, it turns out, is a pretty small town. I'm out with Kira, telling her about *D is for Dan,* my most recent *Match* date: "He seemed like a good fit for me," I say. "Pretty adventurous. He's climbed Mt. Kilimanjaro and his next adventure is Everest Base Camp. How cool is that?"

Kira starts giggling. "Does he sail too?"

I give her an appraising look. "You've gone out with him, haven't you?"

"He never stopped talking!" she says, laughing merrily.

I smile ruefully. It's true. When I saw him waiting for me at the coffee shop, I'd immediately noticed how fit and clean cut he was. The attraction faded as he talked for forty minutes, hardly taking a breath, telling me about his many outdoor and travel adventures; without asking about me at all, he finished up by sharing the story of how he restored his sailboat. It was probably one of the most uncomfortable first dates I'd ever been on.

Kira looks at me questioningly. "Did he stop long enough for you to say anything?"

"No," I laugh. "And I have to admit, I was a bit disappointed. He seemed like such a good fit for me." I sigh and shake my head, "Did you see the picture of his sailboat?"

Kira laughs at me again. "You're so dismissive of men who pose with their cars..."

"Yeah, but a sailboat is totally different."

"Of course it is!" Kira pauses and then adds, "Actually I remember thinking he'd be a good match for you when I went out with him."

"I think I'm going to go out with him one more time. He talked so much that it just had to be nerves. Maybe he'll be more relaxed the next time."

Kira raises her eyebrows. "Nerves? Maybe. Or here's an idea: he might just be utterly self absorbed."

I laugh. "It's so funny that you've gone out with him too!"

But then I have a thought.

"You haven't by any chance gone out with "Born to Fly" too?"

Another shriek of laughter. "The older guy with the plane? Really into *The Four Agreements*?"

I nod.

"Yes!"

"So that means that of the four men I've gone out with so far, you've dated three of them."

"And it's time for you to send Ben my way. That would make it four for four. It seems that I've been generous with my hand-me-downs. Fair is fair."

"No. You can't have Ben. Sorry...He's not a hand-me-down." I'm still feeling horrible about Ben. I know that I've let a good man slip away.

It isn't really a surprise that Kira and I are dating the same men; we are, after all, in exactly the same demographic. But there's still something kind of creepy about the whole thing. I don't really want to have to run past Kira every guy who contacts me, just to find out what he's *really* like.

On the other hand, it might be a useful approach. The reality is that finding a healthy, secure single man in his forties or fifties is not easy. Most of those men are at home with their wives or long-term partners. They're busy in the work of raising families and tending to careers, secure in the knowledge that whatever difficulties arise in their relationships, they can sort them out. And many of the men I've met on dating sites? They're single for a reason. They're men who've spent their lives chasing the next best thing, leaving behind them a string of failed relationships. Or they've placed their own needs first, putting career or travel or self-development before relationships. Some of them are dealing with health or addiction issues. And even the steady, loyal men I've met online are carrying baggage. These are men who end up single because of a partner's infidelity or sudden departure; I know all too well that it takes time to process, forgive and move on from these kinds of life events.

So maybe it's not such a bad idea for Kira and me to pool resources. I run the idea past Kira. "You date all the men with names beginning with A to M. I'll be in charge of the rest of the alphabet. We could weed out the men who fall into the category of 'Absolutely Not.' And those in the category of 'Nice Guy, But Not For Me,' we could pass on to each other."

Kira laughs. "We can call it The Saucy Sisters Dating Cooperative –"

"And we could invite other women to help out!"

"Imagine the spreadsheets we could generate!"

Still laughing, I return to our initial conversation. "So what did you think of Born to Fly?"

"He seemed like a nice guy. Just not for me."

"Uh, hello! He might have been quite lovely, but he also couldn't keep his hands off me. And at the end of the date, he kissed me, even though I was not sending out kissing vibes."

"Ewww! He didn't kiss me, but now that you mention it, he was very touchy and he kept asking me about sex."

"Just for the record, Kira, that memory lapse is a major Dating-Sister infraction! You're going to have to keep better notes!"

But since I'm giving *D is for Dan* a second chance to make a good first impression, I won't need Kira's notes just yet.

In fact, I give Dan two further chances to make that good first impression.

And not just because he has a sailboat.

I find Dan intriguing. I've rarely met somebody with such a clear sense of direction. As he tells me about his life I see that he has identified one goal after the next, and has made those goals happen. Mt. Kilimanjaro? Check. Machu Picchu? Check. Sailboat? Check. I like his sense of focus, his sense of adventure and the fact that he volunteers extensively in his community. He also talks fondly of his closest friends, something I find endearing.

There's plenty to admire about Dan. But there's something that I can't put my finger on that warns me away, an uneasiness I feel around him. As we chat one day over a drink, he says, "Have you hurt your shoulder?"

"No. Why?"

"You've been holding it the whole time we've been here."

I'm leaning forward, my elbows resting on the table, and I'm holding my right shoulder with my left hand. As soon as Dan points it out, I realize I've been sitting like this all the way through the date.

"I used to sit like that when I had an injured shoulder," he tells me. "That's why I wondered..."

"No, my shoulder is fine," I say, a little bewildered.

He looks at me kindly and says, "Perhaps you're trying to protect your heart."

He makes the observation lightly, but it hits me with the weight of truth. That's exactly what I'm doing. I deliberately unfold myself, make a conscious effort to practice open body language, but as soon as we begin talking again, I find myself folding my arm protectively across my chest again.

It's a clear message from my body. Dan, I know, is not for me. No matter how exciting his life is, he is not for me. When I'm honest with myself I can see that he is another in a long line of men who have put their own needs first. It's an admirable trait in some ways. It's what gets them the impressive title, the expensive sports car, the adventurous lifestyle. It's why Dan has travelled so widely and why he has that sailboat. And while I'm drawn irresistibly to men like this, I know that they are not good for me. This time, I want someone who is not so driven, someone who values family and relationships. I want someone who isn't so focussed on himself.

I'm learning to listen both to my heart and my head, learning to integrate that knowing, and finding a place somewhere close, I hope, to wisdom.

And now, here with Dan, that heart wisdom is telling me no. It's a very clear message: *No. Not this one. Not even if he has a sailboat.*

And so, taking Matt's advice, I let Dan see that it's really he who wants to say no.

*Hi Dan,*

*Thanks again for arranging the Flights and Bites afternoon. I really enjoyed trying all the different ports with you. You definitely get double bonus points for coming up with such an inspired idea for a date.*

*If I'd met you three years ago, I wouldn't have thought twice about next month or next year. I would have just let things unfold and waited to see what might happen. But I'm in a more cautious space these days. One concern for me is that we are two people who are deeply invested in our respective communities, and those communities are more than an hour's drive apart. It's fine for dating, but it has the potential to be a big problem for us down the road. And if I'm honest, I suspect that there probably isn't the time in your life for a woman like me. I'm a bit high maintenance. I need quite a bit of time and attention.*

*So, there are my cards, laid on the table for you. And you? How are you doing and what are you thinking?*

*Warm regards,*

*Sally*

# SEVEN

# E IS FOR EDWARD AND F IS FOR FRANK

As spring arrives, the weather begins to warm up. My dating life, however, does not. It is tepid, uninspiring, and slow. I'm finding few potential matches on *Match*, and am beginning to wonder if there are any actual men on *eHarmony*. I hardly ever receive messages through this dating site, and when I occasionally scan through my matches, I'm surprised how few people even have profile pictures.

"It's like a ghost town," I complain to Kira. "I think half those profiles are inactive."

"Yeah, it's pretty quiet compared to *Plenty of Fish*," she agrees. "And you're right. Lots of people just dismantle their profiles and leave them there."

"What's with that?"

"It's like the Hotel California," she laughs. "Good luck getting your profile off that site!"

"Great! So I'll be stuck there forever, getting matched up with people who are probably married. Or dead! And even worse, I'll have to keep dealing with the bozos. One of my matches calls himself Phil McCracken. What kind of an idiot would use a name like that?"

Kira laughs. "I remember Phil! I think I was matched up with Ben Dover too."

I shake my head in wonder. "How the hell did we end up here, my friend?"

I do meet one other man through *eHarmony*, a fit, professional, family-oriented guy who should be a good match. Edward and I arrange to meet for coffee in my own little community. He plans to cycle out to meet me. It's a beautiful, sunny Saturday morning, and when I arrive, Edward has chosen a table out on the street. He's sitting waiting for me, decked out in brightly coloured cycling gear, his thick black hair a bit flattened from wearing a helmet. He's a solid, serious looking man, with a shy smile. Within minutes of sitting down, I can see he isn't for me. He speaks in a dull monotone and doesn't seem to pick up on my humour. I know for sure that I need a man who laughs and who can make me laugh too.

Sitting at a patio table in the sunshine, I also realize the folly of meeting in my own neighbourhood. I've lived in this community for a long time, and it seems that every second person who walks past is somebody I know. I love living in a small community, but not today. I can hardly concentrate, because I'm so preoccupied with who might walk by next. I absolutely do not want to have to introduce Edward to a friend or an acquaintance. Or worse still, one of my kids' friends!

And so I spend the entire coffee date smiling brightly and tossing Edward questions while simultaneously scanning the street for familiar faces. Every time I see someone I know, I hunch down a little in my seat and angle myself as effectively as I can so they won't notice me. I hope I'm doing this in a surreptitious manner.

But I suspect not.

I spend the rest of the day with a churning stomach, feeling horrible about the date. I've treated Edward badly and I know it. Though I like to think of myself as a kind woman who treats everyone respectfully, that's not who I showed up as today. Today I was so worried about what other people might think of me that I couldn't relax and spend an hour just getting to know somebody.

Despite my long experience on Internet dating sites, my date with Edward highlights the fact that I'm still a little mortified to find myself having to do so, and especially at midlife. And it's something I'm going to have to get over if I really want to meet somebody. Though I'm pretty sure that Edward is too serious for me, I know that I was so preoccupied with *what people might think,* that I didn't give him a fair chance.

*Hello Edward,*

*Thanks so much for coming out to my neck of the woods to meet me for coffee yesterday. I enjoyed hearing about your work and your kids, and about your passion for cycling. I appreciated your interest in my world too.*

*It seems to me that we don't share many common interests. I suspect you probably felt that way too.*

*I hope that just around the corner for you is a woman who is wild about cycling and who likes the idea of getting on the back of a motorbike too.*

*Best wishes,*
*Sally*

After Edward, I should know better than to go out with Frank. Though I try to stay open to the possibilities in online dating, there are some men who I'm pretty confident are not going to work out even before I meet them and Frank is one of those men. I can tell that he's probably not for me just from his messages and from his profile picture where he's standing in front of an old Mustang and hoisting a can of beer. But he's insistent, and he suggests a time for a quick meeting that is convenient for me: I'm on my way into town anyway to meet some friends for lunch.

It's another sunny day, and I arrive at the coffee shop in a pretty summer dress and sandals. Frank waves me over to the table he's found. He's wearing a faded Van Halen t-shirt and baggy jeans with holes in them. He hasn't shaved. I'm not sure if he's even combed his hair.

Sometimes it is a really good thing to have low expectations going into a date.

Frank is a mess, and whether I like it or not, I care about appearance. I want to be the sort of person who can look beyond appearance and just see someone's inner beauty, but for me, it's a big ask. I'm sure it's tied to my worries about what other people think, and though I'd love to not care, I do. I just can't see myself on Frank's arm.

I take a deep breath and give myself a stern talking to. *Get over yourself, Sally! Nobody is watching. Nobody is judging. It's just coffee. Give the guy a chance.*

But there are times when first impressions are accurate, and this time is one of them.

*Hi Frank,*

*Thanks for meeting me for coffee this morning. It was interesting to learn a little about your life and career. Who knew that selling car parts could be so much fun?*

*It seems like we have little in common, Frank. I'm not interested in cars and I haven't listened to Van Halen since high school. I'm thinking that you have probably reached the same conclusion about me.*

*Anyway, it was nice to meet you. I hope the right woman walks into your life soon.*

*Sally*

"Am I being too picky?" I ask my counsellor. Linda has seen me through a couple of rounds of dating now. I trust her to tell me the truth.

"There's a difference," she says, "between being picky and being discerning."

Apparently I am discerning.

"I write off men just because they show up for coffee in torn jeans."

"You know exactly what you want," Linda reassures me. "And when the right guy comes along, you'll know."

"When Griff left, he told me not to settle and I keep thinking about that, about what it would mean to settle. I don't want to settle, but I also don't want to hold every man I meet to an impossible standard."

"What would it mean to settle?" Linda asks, echoing my words.

"I don't even know." I pause to think about this. "I guess in some ways, I was settling with Griff, staying in a relationship that wasn't going anywhere."

Linda nods. "Don't worry that you're being too picky. You know exactly what you want."

But do I? I'm not so sure. I think I want commitment, but when I encounter anybody who is really ready for commitment, I can't escape fast enough. Even though I know that I want someone in my life who values family as deeply as do I, I keep finding myself drawn to men who have no interest at all in children. And good luck to any man who isn't handsome and well put together! He won't even get a chance with me.

"Just trust yourself," Linda reminds me. "You know you can trust your inner wisdom."

"Heart and head," I say, smiling weakly. Heart and head. It needs to become my mantra.

My two oldest and dearest girlfriends are sitting together at the table in the cottage we're staying in, gazing together at the laptop screen before them. We have escaped for the weekend to a beachfront resort up island, and all we have planned is to walk the beach, drink wine, and get to the spa.

And since we don't have very much planned, my friends have decided that they will find me a man online.

It doesn't take them long to realize that the pickings are slim. They try on *Match* to find me a man with a similar level of education and salary range, and with at least a few common interests. Not a single match.

It's a bit depressing. But it's also funny to listen to their conversation, these two lovely women, each married for more than twenty years.

"No, he won't do."

"What about this one?"

"Oh, no. Look at his pictures!"

"Tragic!"

"Remember, that's him trying to look his best. Those are supposed to be his *best* pictures!"

"Okay, how about him?"

"Interests: cars, ATV racing, hockey. I don't think so."

"Listen to this profile: 'I'm a happy, healthy male, looking for a nice lady's company.' Spelling errors all the way through."

I nod. "Welcome to my world."

"This is pretty depressing."

"You wouldn't believe the things I've seen," I tell them.

This is why they decide to create a new profile for me on *Plenty of Fish*, where the men are still mostly unsuitable, but because it's a free site, there are more of them from which to choose.

In some ways, it feels like I'm working backwards. I started with a dating site for people who are serious about finding a long-term relationship, until I realized that maybe I wasn't ready for that. Then I signed up for a second site where people have to be serious enough to pay to be on the site. Now I'm signing up for *Plenty of Fish*. It's free and because it's free, everyone is on there. And while I love the crazy, fun, nightclub vibe, I'm just not sure that I'm likely to meet a long-term partner here.

Nonetheless, we get to work building a new profile. We have everything we need: enough wine to fuel our creativity, Kim's iPhone for some new profile pictures, and wireless Internet.

God bless technology.

And so, over the next twenty-four hours, we work on the concept for the profile, brainstorming mostly very silly ideas for how I could best attract the right kind of man. We also get down to the beach to take pictures to accompany the writing, and for the second time in a matter of weeks, I find myself involved in a photo shoot with the express purpose of producing a few good photos for my profile.

By the end of the weekend, we have polished my latest profile, my third dating profile in a matter of months. I am now live on *eHarmony* and *Match*, and I'm ready to launch my *Plenty of Fish* profile.

The three of us admire our work.

*Easily Led Astray*

*You know when you get to one of life's intersections and you're not quite sure where to head next? And you don't have a GPS? And the last copy of "The Lonely Planet's Guide to the Road Less Traveled" has been signed out at the library? I hate it when that happens. But here I am.*

*It would be so much easier if I were thinking about a new profession. I love my work, but if I didn't, I'd consider becoming a weather girl. Ever since I ended up in front of the cameras and diva lights a few years back, I've had this nagging feeling that I missed my calling and that I was supposed to be on television.*

*Or I could become a backup singer. I'm not a particularly talented singer or dancer, but I can rock a little black dress and there's that whole stage and spotlight thing I like so much. When the mood strikes me, I think I'd like to move to Hornby Island and collect sand dollars. It would also be cool to be a National Geographic Explorer in Residence. I could travel to exotic, off-the-beaten-track kinds of places, and write about my experiences. And of course, I've always wanted to be a princess. I'm good wih devotion. And I'm good at giving it back too.*

I end the profile with the "Fine Print" as Matt suggested:

*My three boys still live at home on a part-time basis; the youngest one is 8. I have a handsome ginger tom; if you're allergic to cats, be warned. And I don't kiss on the first date. Ever.*

It takes us a while to agree on what to include in the "Interests" section. Part of me wants to leave it blank, but I know some people actually search based on interests, so I include travel, hiking, kayaking and sailing. And then we throw in a few quirkier details: John Coltrane, Earl Grey tea, and waking up in a tent.

The final step is to write about my perfect first date. I write, *"Gelato on the Spanish Steps."*

A girl can dream, right?

And dream I do. Perhaps this is where I'll meet the one good man I'm looking for.

I wait a couple of days before hitting submit. I know that as soon as I publish my *Plenty of Fish* profile, my life will get a whole lot more complicated.

More complicated. But also more interesting. Within minutes of publishing my profile, the emails start flooding my inbox. Sk8ter Boy 26 has added you as a favourite! Softwherebytes has sent you a message! Dented Armour has added you as a favourite!

I feel a rush of satisfaction. After the deathly silence at *eHarmony*, I was starting to think I'd passed my "Sell By" date. I know that *eHarmony* uses its specialized algorithms to set me up with men who share my values and interests. And if truth be told, the men that I've actually been out with have been better suited to me than the vast majority of men I met the last time I was on *Plenty of Fish*. They've both been lovely: engaging, available, and open. The site does a good job of connecting people with similar values. But two men in two months? Give me a break!

I have to come clean here: I love *Plenty of Fish*. It is my spiritual dating home. I love that there are so many people there and that the men on the site are without inhibition and will send even the most unlikely woman a message, because, hey! You never know! *Plenty of Fish* is the dating site that plays to my strengths and satisfies my deepest need: attention.

If attention is what I'm after, it seems that I've found it. I launch my profile on a Tuesday night. By Wednesday morning, my inbox is full.

And this is the part where you have to have a sense of humour. Because you get attention, there's no doubt. It's just whether that attention is welcome or not.

*Hi Sk8ter Boy 26,*
*I was very flattered that a man twenty years younger than me would notice my profile and contact me. Those are great photos of you at the skateboard park! Unfortunately, I would really like to find somebody who is in the same place in his life as I am.*
*Have fun fishing!*

*Hi Classy Gent,*
*I was very flattered that a man twenty years older than me would contact me. I should have probably mentioned in my profile that my youngest child is eight. Unfortunately, I would really like to find somebody who is in the same place in his life as I am.*
*Good luck in your search!*

*Hi Fun For You,*
*You're right that Chilliwack is too far away, but it was nice to hear from you anyway. I hope you won't take this the wrong way, but I think you might want to change your main profile picture. You should use the other picture of you, where you're zip lining. In that one you look like a fun, adventurous guy. But about your main profile picture: lots of women find pictures of half-naked men a bit unsettling. I'll bet you'd get a lot more responses if you deleted that photo.*
*Good luck and happy fishing!*

So maybe I could be using my time more fruitfully, saving the world or at least posting to my blog, but I don't mind spending a few hours sifting through the emails and writing back to everyone. It reminds me that there are all kinds of possibilities out there, that there is an abundance of men.

And I'm only looking for one.

Fortunately, while I'm waiting, there is much to keep me entertained. This is what I love about *Plenty of Fish*: within twelve hours of posting my profile, with the tagline "Easily Led Astray," I have three men volunteer to lead me as far astray as I want. One particularly enterprising individual offers to lead me to the brink of ruin.

Now what sensible woman could resist an offer like that? This is the note I receive from Desmond:

*John Coltrane?? And you need someone to lead you astray? Well I would love to lead you astray. I have brought many a person to the brink of ruin and I am sure I could work my magic on you, if only you would have me...*

*Now, while you are considering my offer, I think it would be great if you could join my band and sing a few background la la las... especially while rocking that black dress. Remuneration negotiable.*

*Perhaps you could perform a perfunctory profile perusal, and, if there is anything that strikes a chord with you – and you don't find me too hideous or abhorrent –- then this fine fellow, this likely lad, would be most delighted to hear from you.*
*Desmond*

*Hello Desmond,*
*The Brink of Ruin. That is a most tempting offer, a far more interesting destination than Astray. In fact Astray seems dull and pedestrian by comparison! Could I wear the black dress for the occasion? And perhaps a boa? Your message made me laugh out loud and your profile struck a number of pleasing chords. I am so easily led astray by a man who can write. I would have you in a heartbeat if you lived in Victoria. But I have promised myself no men from Vancouver this time. No matter how witty! No matter how charming! No matter how cool their profile pictures are! And the Bartok photo is Brink of Ruin cool. Any chance the UVIC School of Music has just made you an offer you can't refuse and you're on your way to the island?*
*Sally*

*Oh Sally...*
*Now I am at the brink of despair... you can't... you mustn't. It is so very, very rare that a woman would have me in a heartbeat - or even responds - you mustn't cut me adrift.... maybe astray, but not adrift. What if instead of leading you astray or to the brink, I were to take you by hand as we climbed the steps to Parnassus? Nay! I would lead you to the very gates of Elysium. Now rather than ruin, doesn't a life of perpetual bliss appeal somewhat? What if I were to immortalize you in music? The Sally Song? The Sally Sonata? The Sally Symphony? I can... I will... I want to.*

*Anyhow... I wish you the very best,*
*Desmond.*

For all the miseries of Internet dating, an exchange like this keeps me going for weeks. I love the playfulness, the humour, and the wonderful word play. And I realize that a man who writes well can wrap me around his finger in minutes. On a darker note, I wonder whether I'm drawn to sites like *Plenty of Fish* to distract myself from finding a partner. I know that I could spend months flirting with men who, like Desmond, are utterly charming, wickedly funny, and, because they live so far away, completely unavailable.

# EIGHT

# G IS FOR GRIFF

One of the best things about *Plenty of Fish* is the sheer range of people on the site. It's also one of the real drawbacks. While there is enormous possibility for meeting somebody that you wouldn't otherwise meet, there is also enormous possibility for connecting with somebody completely unsuitable. That's what happened with Griff and me. In the small town that Victoria is, we did not have a single connection. We might not have even met the six degrees of separation criteria. We were from different worlds.

When we were first falling in love, we'd marvel that we had found one another. Another miracle of the Internet! But at the end of our relationship, as our many differences came into high relief, I began to question the wisdom of having become involved with somebody so different in values and interests.

In the ugly days of the actual break up, Griff asked me how I could waste so much of my time in fruitless pursuits like reading and writing. "Why spend your time idle when you could be out making money?" He questioned the way I was raising my boys, the cordial relationship I'd crafted with my ex-husband, my inability to keep a tidy house.

The differences piled up, each of us voicing our discontent. "You're too focused on money," I told him. "I just don't care that much about material things." I told him how difficult I found his propensity to think in black and white, my perception that he was inflexible. I admitted how hard it was for me to see the way he treated his ex-wife and his eldest son. That lack of compassion scared me.

But even as we came to see that there was no future for us, the draw between us was strong. Chemistry is a powerful thing.

And continues to be. Even as I try to move on, Griff keeps drawing me back to him. Since that day in March when I'd asked that we not see each other, he's limited our contact to a few business-like emails regarding the renovation and the occasional text. But then suddenly, just after I join *Plenty of Fish*, he sends me a series of texts that leave me reeling.

*I can't get you out of my head.*

*I miss holding you.*

*What we had was magic.*

He also leaves a long, scotch-fuelled voice message. This time, though, I don't feel sad. I don't feel hopeful. I don't feel like calling him just to hear the warm, deep timbre of his voice. This time, something begins brewing in me that feels a little bit like outrage, a little bit closer to actual anger. After months apart, I finally feel strong enough to say no.

*Hi Griff,*
*Thank you for your messages.*
*I have never for a second doubted that you loved me and appreciated me; I know that you worked at our relationship every single day that we were together. I've never doubted that you loved me still the day we broke up. There is a part of me that will always love you for that amazing gift. It's time now, though, for you to let me go. I want to move forward in my life, but the texts and the phone messages are making it really hard for me to do so.*

*Our time together was a wonderful and unforgettable season in my life. But it needs to be over now. Please don't contact me anymore.*
*Sally*

In all the months of firing off "Don't call me, I'll call you" letters, this is definitely the hardest one to write. And it is definitely the one I need to write before I can move forward.

# NINE

# H IS FOR HENRY AND I IS FOR IAN

They say the universe keeps sending us the same lesson until we finally learn it, and after Griff, I am determined to choose my next partner more mindfully. It can't be all about the chemistry, I remind myself, scrolling through the emails on my *Plenty of Fish* account. Life experience matters, I tell myself. Education matters. Politics, family values, interests, they all matter.

Even though there are so many enticing possibilities, I know in my heart that I am probably going to be happiest with a left-leaning, university educated professional, somebody for whom family is a priority and somebody who shares at least a few of my interests. It's time, I tell myself, to look past appearance, and get to know some of the men whose profiles don't exactly excite me, but who fit more closely the profile I know I should be looking at.

With mild foreboding, I respond to Henry, a college professor with a young son. *His profile is so boring!* My inner party girl is protesting loudly. *And it looks like he has a toupee.*

*Stop it,* my sensible side admonishes. *You're just scared to date someone who might share your values.*

Henry responds to my email promptly and his correspondence is respectful and kind if not exactly scintillating. When he proposes that we meet for coffee, I agree, again with little excitement and with that uncomfortable sense of foreboding. Nowhere – not in his profile and not in his emails – do I see any sense of humour. But I know that not everyone communicates best in writing. *You committed to keeping an open heart and an open mind while you dated,* I remind myself. *Give the guy a chance.*

Henry is lovely. Kind, respectful, intelligent. All qualities I know I'm looking for in a man. And deadly dull. I've had my share of coffee dates where the conversation is awkward or stilted and I can see that it's because my date is nervous. But this isn't the case with Henry. He seems absolutely at ease. As we have coffee in an ocean-side café, I struggle to stay focused as he explains in earnest and excruciating detail the intricacies of teaching economics to first-year students, but I can scarcely muster up polite commentary as he drones on. My gaze keeps wandering from Henry and his suspiciously perfect hair to the people walking past the café, heads down and hoods up to avoid the rain. The conversation, I think, is as dreary as the gray day outside. And I'd give anything to pull on my coat, pull up the hood and make a run for it. Some coffee dates can't finish soon enough.

*Hi Henry,*

*It was nice to meet you on the weekend, but I can't see things going any further between us. I wish the chemistry component of this whole dating game wasn't so darn complicated.*

*I wish you well,*

*Sally*

After Henry, I am sorely tempted to respond to Gone Travellin', a rugged looking blond with photos of himself from around the globe. No, he doesn't have children. Or a career. Or any plans to stay in Victoria longer than it will take to put together the funds for his next trip. But he looks so handsome! And interesting! And his profile is charming and funny and well written and I am oh-so-close to giving up on my new commitment to date sensibly.

But no. *Stay the course*, my sensible self reminds me. So instead, I respond to Ian, an engineer who has been left to raise his two teenage daughters after the death of his wife.

We meet first for a walk one Saturday, and talk at length about our families and work, and about the death of his wife. He speaks about her with such love and regard, and about his children with such fondness, that I can't help but like him right away. He is well educated, engaged in the world, and interested in travel; he even lives close by.

There are no fireworks. In fact there is something about him, something I can't articulate, that doesn't feel quite right. But he is open and honest if a bit subdued; we've enjoyed a pleasant time together and found a number of promising points of connection. *Be patient*, I remind myself. *There is potential here even if you don't feel a spark.*

The following weekend we get together again, first for dinner and then to go and see a play. It is over dinner, as he talks a little more about his wife's death, that I recognize the thing that is making me feel uncomfortable: he is still in mourning.

He wants it to be over it. I can see that. He wants to move on. But he isn't ready. Grief takes its own sweet time, as I know too well. I sit across from him, seeing in him what he can't see yet for himself, what I haven't been able to see in myself either. I wonder how many of the men I have sat across from in the past few months have recognized that I, too, was still too sad to move forward.

Ian and I have a pleasant evening, and as the evening ends, he indicates that he would like to pursue this more seriously. I know that I do not. While I could share dinner with him and listen compassionately to the story he still needs to tell, I can see that a relationship is not what he needs just yet. It's not what I need yet either. What we both need is time.

I wish that I had summoned the courage that night to be honest with him and share what I could see in him and what I could finally see about me in his reflection. But I didn't. I fell back on platitudes; fell back on the story I'd been telling every good man I'd met so far.

*Hello Ian,*

*It was nice to see you again the other night. I enjoyed the evening, and really enjoyed getting out to the theatre.*

*As I mentioned the other night, I really need to spend some time dating casually. Although I'd like to be, I don't think I'm ready right now for anything serious. It seems like every time a man starts getting enthusiastic about me, I run for the hills. Thanks again for the other night, Ian, and take care.*

*Sally*

My favourite New Yorker cartoon of all time features a harried-looking man speaking into a telephone. The caption reads, "How about never? Would never work for you?"

Within weeks of joining *Plenty of Fish*, I find myself tempted to write that phrase three or four times a day. After my date with Ian, I've decided that for the time being, I need to date casually, meet lots of men, and just generally have fun. And so I'm trying to leave my *Plenty of Fish* account open for more than twenty-four hours at a time without becoming completely overwhelmed. The trouble is that for every "Maybe" that appears in my inbox, there are three or four "Absolutely Nots."

I understand from my male friends that many women never respond. If they aren't interested, they just ignore the message. But that seems unkind to me. It takes courage to put yourself out there, and I think that anyone who has taken that risk deserves a friendly and kind response, even if in the end that response is still "no thanks".

My rule of thumb is to thank the person for taking the time to contact me, say something nice about his profile, and then give a polite, but firm no. I've learned to be vague. As soon as I give a specific reason, it provides an opportunity for the person to explain why that reason doesn't really matter. It's happened more than once that when I've explained that a man lives too far away, he's responded with, “For you, I'll move to Victoria!" Flattering, but not very helpful.

Sometimes, in the interests of kindness, vague is necessary. I'm still trying to figure out a polite way to say, "I only date men with all their teeth." Or, "I really prefer men who can spell." Or, "I just have a thing about men who pose for their profile pictures fully clothed."

Kira, Queen of All the Internet Dating, ran into a problem recently when she was too specific. After Kira politely declined a twenty-four-year-old's offer to meet, pointing out that he was half her age, her suitor pestered her with reasons why age shouldn't matter. Eventually she sent him this message: "Don't you get it? You are TOO OLD for me! I never date anyone older than twenty-one!" He left her alone after that.

So, I'm pleasant, polite, firm and vague. And if they respond to my "No," I feel no obligation to carry the conversation further. That's what the delete function is for.

The trouble is that this all takes time. I can easily spend an hour every day sending out Internet Dating Rejection Letters, time that could be spent in more purposeful pursuits, such as writing *blog posts* about sending out Internet Dating Rejection Letters.

And so I start fantasizing about ways to solve the problem. Kira and I regularly joke about ways to streamline the dating process. And after reading Timothy Ferriss's *The 4-Hour Workweek,* I come up with an excellent new dating strategy.

Ferriss hires a virtual assistant, who because he lives in India, costs far less than a real personal assistant. Can you see where I'm going with this? I'm going to hire my own personal assistant and have My Man in India take care of all the tedious sorting and all of the diplomatic "No Thank You" messages.

I feel lighter already!

Just about the time when I feel ready to cry about this whole online dating disaster, Kira makes me laugh again. Here's the text she sends me one Friday night: *Would it be wrong of me to accept the offer of a potential suitor's empty condo in Yaletown for the Madonna concert?*

She and I are going to see Madonna in Vancouver, and we need a place to stay.

Yaletown would be perfect. Especially if it were free. But that would mean Kira would have to string along this potential suitor for months. The concert isn't until September. In the world of online dating, that's an eternity.

And Kira's dilemma reminds me of the many thorny ethical issues we face when dating online.

### How many men is it okay to juggle at one time?

I am terrible at juggling men. I've tried it. After two, I start getting confused. Is Ray the engineer or the performance artist? Is Patrick the one who sails and is heading off to Tanzania in September or is that Joe? How many kids does Todd have again? Is it Terry who is the golfer?

If I ran my own dating website, one of the key features would be a spreadsheet, so that I could easily keep track of the pertinent details.

Kira is a master at juggling. I am amazed at the number of men she can simultaneously communicate with and the number of dates she can squeeze into a single week. It is awe-inspiring. But even she gets mixed up from time to time. She recently found herself communicating with two men with the same name, and sent one a message intended for the other. The reply? *I think this email was meant for the other Brian*. Oops.

**How many dates can one reasonably squeeze into a single day?**

Kira is also a master of creative scheduling, and often fits a number of dates into a single Saturday. This approach stresses me out. But I've been known to try it. I once arranged for a 9:00 coffee date with one guy and an 11:30 meeting with another. The dates were in the same neighbourhood, which I thought was excellent planning. There's nothing worse than having to leap into one's car and fly across town between dates. But as I was out for a walk with Date Number Two, Date Number One drove by on his way out of the neighbourhood. Not surprisingly, I didn't hear from Date Number One again.

**After how many minutes of a bad coffee date is it okay to excuse oneself and flee the building?**

Personally, I think abandoning a coffee date is the height of rudeness, but I went out with one man who had this happen to him. Dave admitted to me that he once had a date that was a record ten minutes long. After that, the woman apologized, and then excused herself. I can see how it happened. Dave's profile was hysterically funny, and his emails were witty and intelligent. But the poor man was so nervous meeting me in person that he stuttered all the way through our date.

The second part of the Dave story is that I accepted a second date with him, convinced that we might enjoy ourselves more once the first date jitters were out of the way. He was definitely more confident on that second date; in fact, when our server, who was a former student of mine, asked if we'd like dessert, he replied, "No thanks." Pointing at me, he added, "She'll be dessert tonight."

Um, I don't think so, Dave.

### Is it ethical, under any circumstances, to pretend to go to the washroom, and instead flee the building?

While I don't believe in bolting while on a date, I was sorely tempted the day I met Lawrence for herbal tea. You might remember my story about being trapped in a coffee shop, with a wild-eyed stranger ranting about the Five White Evils.

It is the one time I actually excused myself and made a run for it.

Sometimes the complications of online dating wear me out. And so to Kira's question about the Yaletown condo? I text her back: *Say no. We can afford a nice hotel.*

# TEN

# J IS FOR JOHN

Just as I realize that I need to pull back and keep things light, another keeper walks into my life. John emails me a light hearted and witty introduction through *Plenty of Fish* and invites me to take a look at his profile.

I like what I see. His profile picture shows a tall man with a warm smile standing before the sign of a French winery. His profile is a light-hearted job description, inviting applications for the position of wine-tasting sidekick. John is a researcher, but his true love is wine and he's trained over the past few years to become a sommelier.

I can't resist, and immediately put together my letter of application, citing my extensive experience as a drinker of wine. And thus ensues a playful and quite delightful series of emails during which I establish my credentials as a wino (I mean oenophile) and we learn a bit about one another. John is quite a few years older than I am, nearing the edge of the completely arbitrary age range I've set for myself. His children are grown, and he's considering early retirement to become a working sommelier. Normally, I wouldn't consider somebody nearing retirement. With one child still in elementary school, I'm a long way from retirement myself. But John is devoted to his own kids, doesn't seem concerned about how young my children are, and is planning a second career in Victoria rather than winters golfing in Arizona.

Since I've committed to responsible dating, and to dating only men who I think could be long-term prospects, John is the first man that I feel excited about meeting. He's the first guy who seems to fit all the criteria I've reluctantly identified: he's family oriented, educated, and stable; and he's articulate and very funny. At once I'm excited and scared to meet him: this man, I think, is a real possibility. I know I'll be disappointed if the chemistry isn't there.

It's a sunny morning in May when we first meet for a coffee. He's chosen a funky, independent coffee shop in his neighbourhood and I like him all the more for the choice. He's there when I arrive, sitting at an outside table, waiting with a coffee already in hand. I'm nervous, I realize; my breath is short. But as he stands to greet me, gracious and welcoming, a warm smile on his face, I relax, almost instantly.

"It's lovely to meet you," he says, taking my hand and grasping it in both of his. I like that he doesn't assume that he should hug me, that he is a little more formal in his greeting. And I like the way his eyes crinkle behind his glasses as that warm smile of his spreads across his face. "Let me get you a coffee," he offers. "Sit down. What would you like?"

We sit in the warm sunshine and chat for a couple of hours, a sense of comfort and ease between us from the moment we meet. Though we've emailed back and forth for a few days, we discover other things we have in common and new things to talk about. He is open and honest, disarmingly so. These are traits I find enormously attractive in a man. And the longer we chat, the more I like him.

But I'm not feeling the chemistry. I so want to feel the chemistry with him. This is a man, I think, who could work. This is someone with similar interests and values, someone who would treat me well, someone who would be comfortable in my social circle; this is someone who could connect with my kids and fit into my life. This is a man who would be a very healthy choice for me. I *really* want to feel the chemistry.

I don't hesitate to a second meeting. John and I are so comfortable together, talking and laughing like old friends, moving seamlessly from one topic to the next, finding new connections the longer we talk. But I'm concerned that I don't feel a spark.

Maybe it's fear, I tell myself. Maybe I'm too scared to let myself fall in love with someone like John. Maybe I just need to give it time.

And so we go out a third time, and a fourth. We talk about everything. He tells me all about his kids, about his passion for wine; he tells me about the end of his marriage, about the two relationships he's had since. I tell him about my failed relationships, about my fears of introducing a man into my family. Perhaps unwisely, I also tell him about my dating blog, and in one night, he reads the entire thing and sends me a lovely, thoughtful email about my writing.

But by the end of the fourth date, I have to face the truth: I really like John. I would really love to surrender to this man. But after four dates, I still don't want to kiss him.

*Dear John,*

*Every now and again a man comes along who I know is absolute top quality: you're one of those men, John.*

*I know that you would be an amazing partner. And if I could will myself to fall in love with you, I would have done so already.*

*My heart, I'm afraid, is a capricious creature.*

*I would very much like to cultivate a friendship with you. I thoroughly enjoy your company and would like to continue getting to know you.*

*Sally*

# ELEVEN

# K IS FOR KARL AND L IS FOR LOU

There are times when dating begins to feel like too much hard work, when I am tempted to shut down my profiles and retreat for a while. It's discouraging to ride the hope and disappointment roller coaster too many times. And after John, I am definitely feeling a bit sad, a bit disappointed. I'm questioning my ability to choose a man wisely, because I absolutely know that John would be a wise, healthy choice for me. But even though my head says yes, my heart is not on board.

When Karl contacts me, I'm still feeling discouraged, and even though this new prospect is witty, even though he meets my Responsible Dating Criteria, I can hardly summon up the energy to respond to his first email. Truthfully, I'm hung up on the corporate headshot that he's using as his profile picture. He looks stilted and posed, and it just doesn't work for me. This in itself should be a sign that it's time for a break from dating, but I am accomplished at ignoring these kinds of obvious signals from the universe. But his subsequent emails are playful and there's nothing that I love more than a bit of online flirting, so I go along with it. With little enthusiasm, I agree to meet him one day for lunch. It's so much easier when I go into a first date with low expectations.

And sometimes, even on a date that's going nowhere fast, there's a gem.

"I almost didn't come today," Karl admits over his burger.

"Really? Was it something I said?" I laugh.

"As a matter of fact, yes."

I wait expectantly, wondering whether there is some important dating wisdom coming my way.

"You know how you joked about the boots?"

I nod, remembering an offhand comment I'd made about showing up in stiletto boots. "Oh no. I hope I didn't offend you when I joked about being a dating dominatrix."

Karl smiles. "The last woman I dated turned out to be a *real* dominatrix."

I can't help but laugh, even though my date is looking a little traumatized.

"I had no idea," he says ruefully. "When I went back to the emails after, I could see that she had dropped hints. But I seriously had no idea." He's shaking his head at the memory.

I'm still giggling. "So when I joked about those thigh-high boots, you thought you were two for two!"

He's laughing now. "Yeah! What are the chances, hey?"

I stretch my leg out from under the table to reveal sensible, wedge-heeled sandals. "I think you're safe with me."

Though we have a good laugh about Karl's recent dating misfortunes, there is little else throughout our meeting that feels promising. It leaves me wondering about my new dating approach. So far, I can't say that it's working. And if I'm really honest with myself, I knew before meeting Karl that I probably wasn't going to be attracted to him. I wasn't really drawn to his pictures or his written profile. There was nothing to really spark interest, except that he was a well-educated professional man with children. Clearly there has to be more.

And when I think back, the same could be said for Henry and Ian, neither of whom sparked any more than mild interest in me. What is it about me, I'm starting to wonder, that finds stable professional men with children so unattractive? After all, I'm a stable professional woman leading a life that isn't exactly noteworthy for its excitement. Wouldn't it make sense to connect with somebody, who like me, has personal and professional responsibilities? But no. I keep being drawn to the rugged adventurers who pose at the tops of mountains and aboard their sailboats and in exotic locations throughout the world. What is it about these guys that I find so attractive?

*Hi Karl,*
*It was lovely to meet you. As I'm sure you know, I would never have joked about being a "dating dominatrix" had I known that you were still reeling from your real-life encounter. You just never know who you're going to meet on Plenty of Fish! May the right woman come striding into your life any day now. And may she be wearing sensible shoes.*
*Warmly,*
*Sally*

As summer approaches, I realize I've been violating one of my basic dating tenets, which is that the first meeting should always be super casual and nothing more complicated than grabbing a coffee. This is just common sense. A coffee date is simply a vehicle to determine whether there is interest by both parties in getting to know one another further.

The devil is in the details where online dating is concerned. While a potential suitor may look great on paper, it's not until we meet them in person that we can assess the many intangibles of chemistry. My friend Matt has some very clear rules about online dating. Approach the first meeting with no expectation, he says. Suspend judgment. And don't make any decisions before going out with a person at least three times. That is very open minded of him; however, I beg, to differ. Sometimes you just know, and you know right away. And if it's a big loud no you're hearing, then one date is enough and coffee is the way to go.

So it's funny that I find myself out for dinner at a lovely Italian restaurant with Lou, a man I've never met before, and a man who I'm pretty confident hasn't been entirely truthful about his age. Lou owns a popular restaurant in town, a restaurant that was well established when I came to Victoria at seventeen to attend university. I'm thinking that unless Lou opened his restaurant when he was 12, the numbers just don't add up.

Nonetheless, Lou is a lively and interesting email correspondent and he and I have mutual interests in food, wine and travel. When he suggests dinner, I hesitate, but then decide that even if he is much older, we could have an enjoyable evening anyway. I want to ask him about the cookbook he's writing, about his travels through the US and Europe, and about his early years in the restaurant business.

He is already seated when I arrive, and even in the darkness of the restaurant, I can see that he is much older and much heavier than his profile pictures suggest. But he welcomes me with a smile, gestures for me to take a seat, and asks what I'd like to drink. "There's wine," he says, lifting the expensive bottle of red already open on the table. "Or if you'd prefer something else?"

The wine is perfect and as he pours me some, he says, "There are few things I enjoy more than sharing a meal and a bottle of wine with a beautiful woman." He looks at me meaningfully, and I realize that this is at once an apology, an explanation, and a signal to me that I can just relax and enjoy the evening. I'm not really sure why, but at that moment, I decide to enjoy myself.

Lou is a gracious host and the conversation between us flows easily, from favourite restaurants, to cookbooks, to Lou's early years in the restaurant business, years that must have been gruelling. And yet, he talks about those years with fondness and with quiet humour.

I realize as the waiter clears our dinner dishes that I am really enjoying the evening and happily order coffee in order to extend my time with this interesting man. In communicating that he had no expectations other than a pleasant meal, Lou opened the possibility for the two of us to simply enjoy one another's company. I think about Matt's dating policies, about approaching a meeting without expectation, about staying open, and I realize how much more pleasurable the whole dating experience could be were we to simply decide at the outset to enjoy meeting and not spend the whole time judging and calculating.

As the evening draws to a close, Lou stands up and offers to walk me to my car. I can see that he has some difficulty with his mobility, and I reassess my estimate of his age. But it doesn't matter. It has been a lovely evening, a date that will live long in my memory.

At my car, Lou takes my hand in both of his. "Thank you," he says. "This has been such a pleasure for me." And then he turns, and walks a little unsteadily away.

*Hello Lou,*

*Many, many thanks for the lovely dinner. I can't remember when I've enjoyed an evening so much. You are a true gentleman.*

*Sally*

## TWELVE

# M IS FOR MIKE

For some reason, my date with Lou re-energizes me and I decide that perhaps rather than waiting for men to contact me, I should take the risk and contact one or two men myself. It's easy, I realize, to be on the receiving end of all the introductory emails, to be the one deciding *yes, I'll respond,* or *no, I'm not interested.* It's an entirely different matter to put oneself out there, contact people, and risk rejection.

But I spend some time on the dating website and find a man who appeals to me. He is an attractive and clearly successful man with a well-written profile. If I'm going to be completely honest, his profile picture shows him on his boat. I like to think that I'd contact him regardless, but in the interests of full disclosure, it's a detail I probably shouldn't omit.

It takes me awhile to get up the nerve to email him, to compose the right message. Suddenly, I understand the vague little notes that I sometimes get from men. *"Great profile picture!"*

*"Hi there!"*

*"Looks like you know how to have fun!"*

These sorts of emails always annoy me. How is one to respond? And why, if they are interested, don't they take the time to write something that invites a response?

The answer is nerves.

Now that I'm trying to decide what to say, I realize that the easy thing would be to comment on one of his photos. "What beautiful daughters you have!" But I know that the courageous approach is to take a little more care, to craft a message that identifies some connections we might have and invites him to take a look at my profile. It's harder than you'd think, and all of a sudden, I begin to appreciate the thoughtful and witty introductions that I've received.

Those introductions take time. And guts.

Eventually, I craft a lighthearted introduction that invites a response. I hit send and begin the waiting game.

By the next morning, I still haven't heard a response, and I feel disappointment well up. There's something under the disappointment too. Shame? He doesn't like me! Before I know it, I'm running through all the reasons he might not have responded. Perhaps I'm not pretty enough for him. Perhaps he only dates younger women, or women who are more athletic than I am. Perhaps the fact that I have school-aged kids is a turn off for him. It's shocking how quickly my own insecurities and inadequacies arise. And as I'm going through my own feelings of rejection, I'm aware of how often I've said no to the men who've had the courage to contact me. I'm pleased, at least, to know that I've always responded and thanked them for contacting me. But the message has still so often been "no."

Later that day, I receive a reply. It's a quick email, thanking me for my note and suggesting coffee a couple of days later. It's signed *Mike.* I'm delighted, and doubly nervous now. Again, I'm reminded of how much courage it takes to date online. No wonder some people choose to stay single until someone walks into their lives.

By the time I arrive for our meeting, I've changed outfits three times, and applied and reapplied lipstick. I feel jittery and scattered, and need to take a few deep breaths before getting out of my car. Mike is waiting for me at a table outside the coffee shop, engrossed in a book. He smiles and stands up to greet me. "Sit down," he says, his voice warm and deep. "Let me buy you a coffee. What would you like?"

I watch him as he heads into the coffee shop. He's a handsome man, and well dressed, and he moves with the confidence of somebody who's enjoyed plenty of success in his life. I feel an immediate attraction to him. While I wait, I examine the book he's left on the table. It's a novel about a midwife, a book I've been meaning to read. It seems a surprising choice for a middle-aged man, but I'm impressed. When Mike returns to the table, I ask him about it. "I loved her first novel," he tells me, and we talk at length about the beauty of that book. Not only is he attractive, but also he's cultured and articulate.

Despite how affable he is, I'm nervous, worrying about saying the right thing, and I keep stumbling over my words. As I do in these situations, I keep the conversation going by asking lots of questions. He's relaxed and happily shares stories about his daughters and his ex-wife, with whom he seems to have an amicable relationship. "You should see her little girl," he says, explaining that his ex remarried and had another child. "She's about two now and just adorable. Of course our girls love her!"

I gaze across the table at Mike. Here is a man I could sign on with. He's good looking, successful and intelligent, and I love that he's crafted such an amicable relationship with his ex-wife. But I've been on the dating circuit long enough to pick up the signals. He's pleasant and polite, but not really engaged in the conversation. Whenever someone walks past, his gaze slides away. I can tell that he's not that interested in me.

I'm not all that surprised when he emails me later that day thanking me and letting me know that he didn't feel like we'd be a good fit. I'm not surprised. But I am disappointed and find myself cataloguing once again all the reasons he probably wasn't interested in me.

*Hi Mike,*

*Thanks for your email. It appears that karma is at work in my world. I've been blithely sending out "Thanks, but no thanks" notes on a regular basis, gently letting down one man after another. So I guess I had it coming to me that eventually someone that I was interested in was not going to be interested back. It's a good reminder for me about what it feels like to be the one hearing "no thanks," and how important tact and kindness are in these matters.*

*Thanks again for coffee, Mike. It was good to meet you.*

*Sally*

It's a beautiful, June day and my friend John, the sommelier, and I are driving up island to visit a few wineries. We've decided that even if we aren't going to be a couple, we can still hang out together from time to time.

"I don't know what I'm going to do if this one doesn't work out," John is telling me. He's met a woman who seems perfect for him, a sensual, cultured woman who loves wine and who is ready for a long-term partner. He'd seen her once before, in the local deli, and had been captivated by her then. At the time he didn't have the courage to approach her. And then, lo and behold, he'd found her on *Plenty of Fish*. It seemed like they were meant to be.

I'm really happy for him. Happy and hopeful, and I tell him so.

"How are things going for you?" John asks.

"Karma is at work," I say, and tell him about my recent rejection letter. "I knew it was going to happen sooner or later," I tell him, "but it's so ironic that this was the first guy in a long while that I had that 'Hell Yes' feeling about."

He laughs sympathetically. "We've all been there. But it stings, for sure."

"It really reminded me about being kind when I say no," I say. "Mind you, I sent out a blistering no yesterday."

I'd been emailing back and forth with a local doctor, a man whose every profile picture featured him doing something active and outdoorsy. In one he was at the top of a mountain, snowy peaks fading away in the distance. In another he was ice climbing. A third photo featured him, posing with his dog on his sailboat. Though he was clearly not sensible dating material, I was drawn to his sense of adventure. He'd been emailing every day, and then he just suddenly disappeared. For two weeks. Yesterday, he'd emailed me and picked up the conversation as though there had been no break. No explanation. No apology.

"Can you believe that kind of behaviour?" I ask John, my voice taking on a bit of an edge.

John shakes his head, again expressing sympathy with my plight. "So what did you tell him?" he asks.

"I wasn't very nice," I admit. "I said something like, 'You might have missed the part in my profile about me being a princess.'"

John is laughing out loud.

"And then I explained that I'm the kind of girl who expects regular attention and that I didn't think he was the sort of guy I wanted to date."

John is laughing even harder. "Wow. You didn't mince words."

I laugh. "I'm a bit embarrassed really. It was a little over the top. But at least he could have said, 'I'm heading out of town' or 'sorry I haven't been in touch.'" I sigh dramatically. "It's too bad. He had a nice looking sailboat."

John looks at me, a little surprised. "Doctor, right?"

I nod.

"Was there a dog in any of the pictures?"

"Yep. A black and white one, maybe a collie? Why?"

"Was this guy's name Eric, by any chance?"

I look at John in surprise. "How do you know that?"

He shakes his head. "You dodged a bullet with that one." John explains that a friend of his had dated this particular man and had come by his place one day to find him in bed with another woman.

"Oh my gosh! Victoria is such a small town, hey?"

He nods. "It really is. I can see why he'd have been attracted to you, though. You and Meg are both outdoorsy, both petite and pretty."

I'm still musing about how unlikely it is that John would know someone who had contacted me, and I'm only half paying attention as he starts talking about an old girlfriend who has since married.

"You should see her little girl," he says. "So cute. She just turned two."

Something's ringing a bell and I'm sitting up a little straighter, listening carefully.

"What's your old girlfriend's name again?" I ask.

"Elaine."

"And her ex-husband is Mike, right?"

Now it's John's turn to look at me. "Right."

"Mike's the guy I went out for coffee with, who sent me the thanks but no thanks email!"

There's a moment of absolute silence.

"And you liked him?" John sounds stunned. "I can't believe that you could go out with me and also go out with a guy like him!"

I laugh. "Elaine obviously did."

"Yes, but she was young when she met him. Sally, he's such a lady's man. I can't believe you couldn't see that." John goes on to catalogue Mike's many affairs and indiscretions.

Now it's my turn for silence. How could I not have seen it? I like to think that I have good dating radar, but apparently not. Mike is truly the first man in a while that I felt an immediate attraction. It's one more thing for me to meditate on. Why would I be so drawn to a man who would have been so bad for me?

After a while, John says, "You're pretty lucky, you know. You've dodged two bullets this week."

Indeed.

## THIRTEEN

# N IS FOR NATE

Though I can laugh about my small-town dating adventures, I'm troubled after my conversation with John. Why is it, I wonder, that I am so drawn to men who aren't good for me? Why do I keep gravitating to the high-flying executives, the adventurers, the freedom seekers? Why do I keep choosing men who will always put their own needs and desires first? Why am I, at heart, so attracted to selfishness? I wish I could understand this about myself. And I wish I could come to really appreciate the good, steady, loyal men who are out there and who I keep turning down.

I grew up with a father who was one of those good, steady men, and I married someone who I thought embodied those same qualities. You'd think that this would be my default. But I think after my marriage ended, I stopped trusting men. The stable, loyal ones were a threat. They'd only hurt me in the end. They'd eventually leave me. Better to choose the men I could count on to be self-serving from the start. Somewhere along the way, I'd lost faith in myself, and stopped trusting myself to choose wisely.

Deep down I know I need to find someone I can trust, and so I stick to my strategy of dating men who appear to be solid and steadfast. Chasing excitement is not a dating strategy that's working for me. So with heavy heart, I head out to meet Nate. I'm not even sure why I said yes to coffee, except perhaps because I'm questioning my ability to screen potential partners. Nate has three teenagers, he loves country music, and he dreams about retiring to somewhere warm. None of this interests me. In fact, there is not one thing in his profile or in the messages we've exchanged that sparks in me any sense of excitement.

I realize I should have trusted my instincts on this one the moment I see him. Nate is a paunchy man in need of a haircut and some fashion advice. He's sporting a patterned acrylic sweater right out of the eighties and I know immediately that this is not a man for me. I know that I started out with the resolution to keep an open mind while dating. But that acrylic sweater is too much for me. I briefly consider ducking out before he sees me, but too late. He smiles and waves.

I am committed.

I smile my sunniest smile and give myself the pep talk. *It's just a walk. You don't have to marry the guy.*

Which is a good thing given the complications of Nate's life. As we walk, he tells me about the trouble his two older kids have had with the law and the troubles the youngest is having in school. I have to appreciate Nate's honesty, but it isn't a pretty picture. It's going to take a special woman to walk willingly into that situation. And I am definitely not that kind of special. I've never been much interested in rescuing other people and the longer I listen to Nate's story, the more anxious I am to escape.

As I'm driving home, I realize what a mess I'm getting myself into by second guessing my judgment. I've been trying so hard to date sensibly and keep an open mind about the men I'm meeting online that I'm ignoring my instincts. I knew from Nate's profile picture that I didn't find him attractive. And if there's one thing I should know by now, it's that appearance matters to me. Regardless of how this reflects on me, it's time to give up the fantasy that I'm completely open minded. Turns out I'm not. It's time to accept that I want an attractive partner, and date accordingly.

*Hello Nate,*

*It was nice to meet you and find out a little more about you. Truthfully, I can't see how you and I could make things work together. We both have complicated home lives and responsibilities that will continue for a good many years. Sometimes timing*

*decides things for us. I hope that the right woman appears in your life soon.*
*Sally*

Shortly after meeting Nate, Kira and I are having coffee, catching up with each other. We've already covered work and our respective children, and now we're on to recent dating escapades. I'm telling her about the man I'd been out with earlier that week. "You wouldn't believe how complicated his home life is, Kira. His wife picked up and left him with three teenagers. He seems really nice, but it sounds like complete chaos at his house. Two of the kids have been in trouble with the police. One ran away..."

"Oh, yeah! Nate," Kira says. "I went out with him too."

I look at her with shocked surprise.

"Yeah, way too complicated. You don't want to get involved with him."

"I wish I'd checked in with you before," I laugh. "I could have saved myself an awkward afternoon!"

But our exchange gives me an idea. Later that night, I fire off an email to Kira with thumbnails of three men who have recently contacted me. The accompanying message is concise: "Have you dated any of these men?"

She phones me almost immediately: "Oh My God! Number One is the crazy Cat Man!

Kira went out with the Crazy Cat man a few months earlier and had regaled me with her stories about the high-strung, cat-breeding, recovering crack addict. Thanks, but no thanks, Crazy Cat Man!

Number Two, she tells me, is actually about eighty. While I have recently enjoyed a very pleasant evening with Lou, the man who lied magnificently about his age, I don't want to make this a habit. Sorry, "Eighty," but I just can't see things working out for us.

"I don't recognize Number Three," Kira tells me. "You're good to go with him."

"This is so great!" I enthuse. "You're saving me so much time and energy!" I pause for a moment, thinking. "Hey, Kira, why don't I send you Number Three's profile and you can check him out for me too?"

"No way, sister! You have to pull some weight here. I dated Number One and Two. It's your responsibility to go out with Number Three.

Damn!

# FOURTEEN

## O IS FOR OLIVER AND P IS FOR PETER

As June slips away, I feel despair settling over me. I know I'm disheartened by the hope-disappointment loop and I'm discouraged that I still haven't met somebody. It dawns on me one day that I have just assumed that by the summer, I would have met the right guy. It took about five months of online dating to meet Griff, and somehow, I realize, I've had that arbitrary five-month deadline fixed in my head this time too. As that five-month mark looms, I have to face the fact that this whole process might take longer, a fact that sends waves of exhaustion through me. It's time for a break.

The trouble with online dating though, is that the process takes time, and there are a few men with whom I've been corresponding, who I'd like to meet. Despite my despair, I am an optimist. I can't help but think, what if this is the one?

And so I meet Oliver, a lawyer, for coffee. I'm uneasy about this date, because I have a long history of driven, ambitious men, and while I am drawn to this type, I'm beginning to understand that I might be happier with someone who places relationships and family before money. That slacker, surfer dude that I'd joked about when I first found myself single? He's beginning to look more appealing.

As Oliver pulls up to the coffee shop in his red Porsche convertible, it's clear that "slacker" isn't in this man's repertoire. But every one of his profile pictures shows him playing: traveling in the developing world, kayaking, surfing, hiking. He clearly doesn't subscribe to the "All Work" philosophy and so, as he strolls in, I repeat once again my dating mantra. *Stay open. Don't judge. Just enjoy yourself.*

Oliver is charming and boyishly handsome, and he has that captivating confidence of a man who has enjoyed success in his life. We talk about our travels and our work, and I'm flattered that he seems genuinely interested in what I do. As he tells me about his work as a trial lawyer, I see that he is highly driven and very busy. When he tells me how many cases he's currently working on, I ask, "How do you have time to breathe?"

He laughs. "The junior lawyers do all the heavy lifting," he says, and he moves on to his recent interest in kayaking to assure me that he has time in his life.

It's when we begin talking about our relationship histories that the red flags go up. He describes his ex-wife with unusual venom and he communicates a cynicism about relationships that is disconcerting. At one point, he sighs. "I don't even know why I bother with trying to find someone. It never works out. And in the end it always feels like women are just after my money."

I'm tempted to share my concerns about meeting him precisely *because* of the money, but I decide against it. He wouldn't believe me anyway.

*Hi Oliver,*

*Thanks so much for coffee yesterday. My sense is that we see relationships from very different perspectives. I am an eternal optimist, convinced that should I find the right man, and should I work hard enough at the relationship, I might still have a chance at happily ever after. You seem pretty convinced that happily ever after is an illusion. With such different perspectives, I can't see that it could work for us.*

*Sally*

In the strange way that the universe works, the very next man I meet is *training* to become a lawyer. You'd think that given Oliver's comments about the junior lawyers doing all the work, I'd have given Peter a miss, but his emails were sweet and intelligent and he talked about his young daughters with such affection that I couldn't say no.

Peter is an attractive man, soft spoken and gracious, and I like him immediately. But as he tells me about his life, about his full-time job and his part-time parenting responsibilities and law studies, I see that he does not have a moment for himself. Where, I wonder, could he possibly squeeze a relationship into this already over-packed life?

*Hello Peter,*
*It was nice to finally meet you this weekend. I enjoyed our conversations about education and parenting and following one's dreams. Peter, though I enjoyed our conversation, I just can't see that you could have time in your life for a girl like me. One thing that I know absolutely for sure about myself is that I need a fair bit of attention. With your busy life, you need a woman who will be far less demanding than me. I wish you well in your pursuit of knowledge and in your pursuit of love.*
*Sally*

Though I'm a bit discouraged, I'm happy that I've at least been out on a couple of dates with men who I've found attractive and interesting. Accepting that I'm so appearance-driven is hard, but it's a relief to be honest with myself. I remind myself that each coffee date I go out on is a learning experience. After Oliver, I'm reminded that I need somebody who believes still in happily ever after. After Peter, I'm reminded that I really want someone who has time in his life for me. Even if neither man has turned out to be a good prospect, they've both been interesting people. I've enjoyed meeting both of them and enjoyed finding out about their lives. If nothing else, they've helped clarify a few more things that are important to me in a partner.

But even as I'm reminding myself about all that I'm learning through online dating, even as I'm telling myself that every no is getting me one step closer to yes, I'm truthfully starting to get a little concerned.

*The Alphabet Dating Game* seemed like a good idea when I started out. But here I am a few months in, and I'm getting dangerously close to Z, without a good prospect in sight. I remember breezily declaring that I'd at least have to get to *S is for Stefan* before I found a keeper, but here I am at *P is for Peter* and things are not looking promising. I am a mere ten dates away from the end of the alphabet! What happens if I get to *Z is for Zach* and I'm still playing catch and release? Then what?

I suppose I could start on the Cyrillic alphabet, though I'd have to figure out how to meet men living in Bulgaria and Belarus. And of course there are all those Japanese and Chinese characters. But what an awful lot of effort just to document my dates! Really, I should just have given them numbers. There is beauty in the infinite.

The real issue here is that I haven't met anyone who feels right for me. They've all been nice enough. I haven't gone out with a single man who is crazy. Every one of them has seemed reasonably well adjusted. Actually, many of them have seemed to be remarkably together, responsible and respectful people. They've all been gainfully employed; indeed, many have been very successful, driving luxury vehicles, or owning toys like sailboats. I've dated a number of very good-looking, athletic men, men who I'd be delighted to be seen with. I've met a number who have impressed me with their commitment to living their dreams, who are climbing mountains and traveling to remote corners of the world and completing advanced degrees, who are living Carpe Diem everyday. I've met a number who seem like wonderful, thoroughly decent, happy individuals, men who I know would be really good partners. But I haven't met anybody yet that both my head and my heart can agree on.

And what I'm starting to wonder is what's wrong with me? Have I become the choosiest woman on earth? Have I developed a dangerously over-inflated sense of myself? Have I begun to discard men without giving them a fair chance, secure in the knowledge that there are plenty more out there? I think it's one of the dangers of online dating sites like *Plenty of Fish*. It's easy to become cavalier, to rule men out, to move on to the next promising profile without taking the time to get to know the last person at all. And I don't think that it's just women who are doing this, though I suspect we may be the guiltier sex.

As I recognize the growing despair and growing cynicism in myself, I know that I really need to take that break I've been thinking about. I need to shut down my profile and get offline for a while. I need to recharge.

And I will, I promise myself, as soon as I've met *Q is for Quinn* and *R is for Richard*: they just seem too interesting to say no to.

# FIFTEEN

# QUINN, RICHARD, AND STEFAN

At this point, I know I shouldn't be dating. All the signs are there: I'm sending out curt "No thanks" messages to just about every man who contacts me; some of the messages I'm receiving, I'm just deleting, without responding at all; and most telling, I've completely abandoned my "Responsible Dating" guidelines.

Remember how I was only going to date men who were family oriented, who were the sort of men who could fit into my whole life? Somehow, I've lined up dates with two men, neither of whom has ever been married, and neither of whom has any interest in kids.

But I am such a sucker for a well-written introductory email! And when someone establishes a playful, edgy and intelligent correspondence with me, I am completely captivated. Which is how I find myself going out with Quinn, a communications specialist. We go out together not once, but twice. I know Quinn is completely unsuitable for me before I meet him the first time. He makes it clear in his profile that he is only interested in dating casually, he loves the downtown, urban lifestyle, and he's actually considering relocating to Toronto. But that's okay! How can I resist a man who refers to me as "The Girl in the Black Dress?" How can I say no to a man who gamely takes on the persona I bestow upon him, "Boy Genius?" And when I meet him, he is so interesting and quirky and *wrong* for me that I can't help but say yes to a second date.

It's only after our second date that we both come to our senses. He meets me one afternoon for drinks in my neighbourhood, in my sleepy little seaside town, inhabited mainly by senior citizens and young families. We sit in the ocean-side pub, watching the world go quietly by, and he shakes his head and actually says, "I had no idea that people lived like this!" I can't help but laugh, not just at his reaction, but also at my own delusions where men are concerned.

*Hello Quinn,*

*Thank you for your lovely note. I've never had such a gracious "No Thanks" in my life! I'd been planning to write something along the same lines to you, but hadn't yet found the words. Your note was such a pleasure to receive. Honestly, I wish every man on Plenty of Fish had to take a course from you on good grace and good manners.*

*You're absolutely right that you are too unconventional for me. No matter what else, there is an important part of my life that is suburban soccer mom, and that's not going to change any time soon. Much as I'd love to give free rein to my free spirit, there are responsibilities in my life that I take very seriously.*

*I hope that the right woman arrives soon in your life.*

*With respect and affection,*
*I remain,*
*The Girl in the Black Dress*

Fast on the heels of my dates with Quinn, I find myself out with another charming and unsuitable man. I'm down on Victoria's inner harbour, with Richard, watching the Canada Day fireworks. The atmosphere is festive and fun, the huge crowd roaring in appreciation as the fireworks light up the night sky. As the last explosions echo through the city, and as the last of the enormous red and white fireworks bloom across the sky and then slowly drizzle into night, I turn to look at my date and think to myself, "What the hell am I doing here?"

Don't get me wrong: Richard is sexy, successful and very charming, the sort of man that my father used to say "could sing the birds from the trees." We've spent the whole afternoon and evening together, starting with a walk along the waterfront, followed by an impromptu dinner at a little wine bar in his neighbourhood, and then followed by Richards's invitation to take in the fireworks. I love that kind of spontaneity, that sense of adventure and fun.

So really, I am having a great time. I've spent the whole afternoon and evening talking and laughing, enjoying Richard's humour and his attention.

I'm drawn to men like Richard. I'm drawn to confidence and charisma. I love a man who is saying yes to his life, moving to Victoria because he likes the idea of living in this city, buying a Harley because he's always wanted a motorbike. And even as the red flags are going up, I'm still thinking, "Yes, but he's so hot!"

This is a man who is wrong for me in so many glaringly obvious ways. The longest relationship he's ever had is a couple of years; he has no children and no interest in children; he's very focused on himself; and it's clear that he has a "my way or the highway" mindset. Not long-term material at all, at least for me. But still I'm drawn in.

So here I am, watching the fireworks with this fun-loving and charismatic man, and wondering at the irony of the situation. I've been thinking about fireworks for a while now. I've been thinking in particular about how much store I put into "chemistry," into that initial connection and attraction I'm looking for when I meet someone. I don't think I expect fireworks. But I do want a spark. And there's definitely a spark with Richard. The trouble is that I'm pretty sure that chemistry is an impulse I cannot trust.

Even if I know that the draw of chemistry is dangerous, I'm still choosing spark over substance. I've just ended email correspondence with two men on *Plenty of Fish*, both of whom seem like thoroughly decent, good guys. These are both men who have track records of long, stable relationships, men who appear to value family, who profess the importance of loyalty and fidelity. They both have stable lives, good careers, and, as far as I can tell, well adjusted adult children. If I really want a long-term commitment, why am I not giving these men a bit more of my time? It's just that they seem a bit boring. Nice, but dull.

Apparently, I'm not interested in nice. I'm not interested in long-term and stable. Apparently, I'm looking for a bad boy on a motorcycle, someone who will whisk me away on a spontaneous adventure, who will sweep me off my feet with romance, and then disappear when he starts to feel trapped by the commitment. Apparently I'm looking for the short-term excitement of fireworks rather than the slow burn of a small fire that might warm me for years.

What I really want to know is whether it's possible to have both.

*Hey Richard,*
*It was really fun to meet you the other day. I had a great evening with you, and enjoyed your good humour and upbeat energy.*

*I suspect that you are the kind of guy around whom parties just spontaneously break out.*

*In fact, I'm pretty certain that it would be "all fun, all the time" with you. And if I were in a different place in my life, I'd be lining up to go out with you again. But even though I joke about finding a bad boy on a motorbike, I think that I'm looking for something different in my life right now.*

*I can't imagine that a man like you will be single for very long. I hope that a sexy and successful Harley-riding, party-loving girl blasts into your life before too much longer.*

*All the best,*

*Sally*

After Richard, I find my way back to my therapist's office. It's a little troubling how much time I spend with her these days. "What's scary," I say, "is that I don't trust myself right now."

Linda nods her head, and in that infuriating, therapist way, waits for me to keep talking.

"I used to have such faith in my gut," I continue. "I used to trust in my own deep knowing."

She nods again and waits some more.

"But now it seems like I'm attracted to all the wrong guys, guys who would be perfect if all I wanted was some fun." I tell her about Richard, my bad boy on the motorcycle.

"What is it that you really want, Sally?"

"I don't know! The responsible parent part of me wants to find somebody who's kind and loving. And stable." I laugh at myself as I start thinking it through. "But the free spirit part of me is bored by all that. She just wants to have some fun."

I look at my therapist, who is nodding and smiling a bit. "Head and heart," she says. "It's a familiar theme for you."

It's my turn to nod. When will my head and my heart ever learn to communicate? I wait for her to go on.

"What you've been working toward is integration, right?"

I nod again.

"You want to find ways to integrate your responsible, parent-self and your fun-loving, free-spirit self. They're both critical aspects of who you are."

I nod some more, feeling myself starting to cry.

"Think about the complexities of your character. There are men out there who are just as complex, men with adventurous spirits who also value family. I see men like this all the time in my practice."

I laugh. "You should run a dating service!"

She laughs too, and then continues. "It's not an either/or proposition, Sally. You don't have to choose fun loving at the expense of family. Or the other way around. You can have both."

"In one man?" I'm trying for another joke, but she's not laughing.

"In one man." She pauses and then continues. "Summer's started now. You've got some time away from work."

I nod, wondering where this is going.

"What are you longing for this summer?"

I take a deep breath and let the question echo inside me.

"Freedom," I say. It's the first word out of my mouth, and it surprises me. "Adventure. Fun." I pause, waiting to see if there is anything else. What am I longing for? "Time," I add. It's just floated up into my consciousness.

I look at Linda for a long moment, letting the words sink in.

"I really shouldn't be dating right now."

She just nods her head and smiles her inscrutable therapist smile.

After my meeting with Linda, I email a few men I've been chatting with to tell them I'm taking a break and then I shut down my various dating profiles.

Then I compose one final note, to Stefan, a single dad who I've had coffee with twice. My head says yes about Stefan. He's a professional man who is dedicated to his kids and to his various volunteer commitments. "At least get to know him," my head very sensibly says. But my heart has been sending an equally clear message: "No!"

*Hi Stefan,*

*I'm sorry I've been so intermittent in my communication this week. I am struggling with the whole dating thing at the moment and think that I need to take some time away from it.*

*I have really enjoyed our meetings and wish I were in a different space. I can see that you are a man with much to offer in a relationship. I really hope that you meet somebody soon who is perfect for you and who is ready to take that big leap.*

*Maybe I'll see you on the soccer field in the fall when our kids play against each other again.*

*Take good care, Stefan.*

*Sally*

As I hit send, I feel relief wash over me. It's definitely time for me to take a break.

# SIXTEEN

# A SUMMER INTERLUDE

The relief I feel in getting off the dating sites is short-lived. Within days, it's supplanted by a sense of restlessness, a mild anxiety I can't quite place. I've got more time now, but it's not just that. It takes a while for the understanding to float to the surface, and as it does, I find myself, once again, facing some uncomfortable truths about myself. My search for love through the spring has been an escape from sadness, and it has also been a way to avoid facing my greatest fear: the fear of being alone.

It's a very particular kind of alone that I'm afraid of. I'm actually very good at standing on my own two feet, of providing love and stability and sustenance for my children, of taking care of my finances and paying the mortgage. I can shovel the driveway when it snows. I can even power wash. During our years together, Griff and I always maintained separate households. I'm perfectly capable of doing certain kinds of alone. In fact, I could make an argument that I've been doing alone pretty successfully for a very long time. In the last ten years of our marriage, my ex-husband was on the road more than he was home. I was adept at running the household on my own, parenting alone, and socializing without him.

Yes. I can do alone like nobody's business.

But the kind of alone that scares me, the kind that wakes me up in the night, is a kind of existential loneliness. It's a sense of being without mooring, of lacking safe harbour. It's that terrifying understanding that it's just me, all alone. It's the knowing that with freedom and independence comes complete responsibility for myself.

I don't know why this is such a scary place for me, but it is. And I suspect I'm not alone. I remember asking *B is for Ben* what he wanted most in a relationship. "I want to grow old with somebody," he told me, in his characteristically open way. "I want to know that there will be somebody there to bury me when I die."

But even if this fear of being alone is widespread, it's still something I need to address. I can see how it hampers me in relationships, how it keeps me in relationships well past their "sell by" dates, and how it creates anxiety in me when I feel a partner pulling away.

And so even though I don't like being alone, I decide it's time for me to try it for a while. As the summer starts, I decide to spend some time getting comfortable with being on my own, with not being in a relationship, with not even looking for a relationship. I need to gain distance and perspective, not just on my last relationship, but also on my whole way of being in relationships. I need a break in order to get centered.

Without the dating to keep me busy, I can see that my quest for "The One" has really just been a way of not facing the lingering hurt over the ending of my relationship with Griff. When I look back at my springtime dating frenzy, I see that I've been looking for somebody to take care of me. I've forgotten again that I need to take care of that responsibility myself. It shouldn't be such a surprise, but it is. I know I haven't taken good care of myself over the last few months, at least not in a way that nourishes me and brings me alive. And so, as summer begins, I return to the questions that help me to be true to myself. I return to the practice of asking myself, "What do I want? What fills me up? What brings me joy?

I pull out my calendar, and start scheduling in small adventures through July and August with my boys: a number of camping trips and a couple of day trips to some of my favourite places. I mark the weekend we're going camping with three other families for a long weekend, a summer tradition we all love. And as I fill in the calendar, I feel my anticipation rising. Already the summer ahead is feeling more enticing, more adventurous. Scanning the calendar I realize that I've already started building in those things I wanted out of the summer, the things I identified with Linda: I've got time, some little adventures, lots of freedom. I've got fun. All of these, I know, are things that make me feel whole.

I also realize that this is likely why I've been so drawn to the adventure-seekers. Perhaps I haven't had enough adventure in my own life and so I've been looking for someone to provide the adventure for me. It isn't a comfortable thought.

With my boys on school holidays, we settle into the slower rhythms of summertime, enjoying hikes and beach time and time in the backyard. And as I begin to settle into the summer, I remember how delicious it is to have time and space just for me. I have so much more time when I'm not on the dating sites and not squeezing coffee dates into my already busy life. But it's more than that. I have released myself from the emotional pressures of dating too. It's not until I stop that I realize how much psychic space this kind of venture requires.

As I relax into this new place, I find myself returning to the things I love. Evenings when I would have been on the dating sites are now devoted to long walks and hours of journal writing. Saturday mornings, when the boys are with their dad, when I might have been sitting down to coffee with another new prospect, are now spent having coffee with friends or exploring one of the local farmers' markets. Within a week, I feel calmer, more centered. This, I realize, is what healthy feels like.

In the funny way that the stars sometimes align, I get another offer of adventure in early July. I'm having a coffee with *D is for Dan*, as we do from time to time. Dan is one of the adventure seekers I met early on, the outdoorsy one who'd climbed Mt. Kilimanjaro and hiked to Machu Picchu. I'd admired his sense of adventure and his sense of purpose, but I knew that he was not the right guy for me. Nonetheless, Dan and I check in from time to time and commiserate about our respective dating experiences.

"I'm taking a break from the whole dating scene," I tell him. "I so need a break. It's making me crazy right now."

Dan laughs. "It'll do that to you."

"It's time for me to slow down and take care of myself, time to do some of the things I love."

Then Dan makes me a very tempting offer. "If you've got the time, why don't you come out sailing with me a couple of times this summer?"

Have I mentioned how much I love sailing? I grew up around the water and have a life-long love of the ocean, and the only thing for me that is better than being near the ocean is being out on it, preferably on a sailboat. I am, I suspect, part mermaid.

My free-spirit self is practically doing cartwheels. *Yes! Yes! Say yes!*

But my responsible self is not so impressed. *Hello? No dating? Remember? And you know already that Dan is not the guy for you.*

Responsible self wins, and I decline Dan's offer. "Thank you. I'd love to sail with you this summer. But we both know that we're not meant to be together." I begin listing off the reasons. "We're in such different places in our lives. We're too attached to our respective communities..."

Dan interrupts me gently. "I'm not asking you to go out with me. I'm asking you to come out sailing. Think of it as having a coffee with me on the water."

Free spirit self is now doing back flips. *Yes, Yes, Yes!*

"Oh, I don't know," I say, trying to think the matter through.

"Look, there's no pressure," Dan says. "Just think about it."

I nod. "Okay. How about if I get back to you?"

He smiles. "You just finished telling me that you wanted to spend the summer doing the things you love and I know that you love sailing."

I laugh. "Actually, what I love is being on the water with a gin and tonic watching the sunset. But my preference is to be on a sailboat while doing so."

"We could arrange for that," Dan smiles. After a pause he says, "The timing is good. I've got a bit of time off. You're not tied up with dating. Think about it."

I smile. "Okay, I'll think about it."

"You weren't having any fun dating, were you?"

I shake my head.

"When are you going to let yourself have some fun, Sally?"

A couple of weeks later Dan and I are out on his sailboat, watching the sun set over southern Vancouver Island. "Are you having fun yet?" Dan teases as he hands me a gin and tonic. The evening is warm and there's hardly any breeze. Sidney Spit stretches out behind us, a long thin strip of sandy beach, and beyond that Mt. Baker shimmers pink in the distance. I am in my element. I love being on the water, feeling the salt tang of the air and listening to the muted sounds drifting from boats moored nearby. It is so peaceful here, and so beautiful.

It's a Tuesday night, a work night, but Sidney Island is close enough that we can motor out to watch the sunset and get back before darkness falls. Even though we're only out on the water for a few hours, I feel my cares slipping away and notice for the first time in a while a sense of deep satisfaction. It's a long time since I've felt this way and it feels really good.

I'm back on Sidney Spit within a week, packing a picnic lunch and taking the little foot passenger ferry over to the island with my boys. Even at 9:00, the sun is hot on our faces and the ocean breeze is inviting.

"Come on you guys!" David leads the way through the forest trail and out toward the beach. He's carrying the backpack with our lunch in it. Gavin is in charge of the soccer ball and a bag of beach towels. Luke holds my hand and clutches his beloved stuffed cat in his other hand. We walk a little more slowly, watching his brothers race ahead. I squeeze his hand and smile at him. He gives me a big, happy grin and begins telling me a little story. And in that moment, I feel absolutely whole and contented.

# SEVENTEEN

# SEX AND THE SINGLE KAYAK

The one thing that is worrying me as the summer progresses is the two-week blank on my calendar at the beginning of August. The boys will be away with their dad and I will be on my own. I am not working and have nothing planned. Most of my friends will be away on their own holidays at that time and that blank space feels a little frightening to me. Having a day or two on my own is one thing. I love short periods of solitude and silence. But two weeks entirely alone? I'm at a loss about what to do.

There is one brave and possibly misguided part of me that wants to leave that blank space completely blank, to force myself into spending two weeks on my own. Sometimes I need to step into the places that scare me the most in order to show myself how strong I actually am. But being entirely on my own and entirely without plans scares me to death.

So when Matt calls me and tells me that he really needs an adventure over the summer, I pipe up right away: “I’m your girl!” And then I suggest a time during those first two weeks of August. Really, there’s no point in deliberately forcing myself into two weeks of misery. And one can never have too many adventures.

This is how Matt and I end up on a four-day kayaking trip in the Broken Islands.

"Okay," our guide says, "for today, we'll put the couples into the doubles kayaks. Matt and Sally, you take this one."

I look at Matt, mild panic bubbling up. They think we're a couple! But before I can clarify that the two of us are just friends, the guide has moved on, assigning the other members of our group to kayaks. In retrospect, I should have spoken up right away, because after that it’s difficult to find the right time or place to announce, "Oh, and by the way, Matt and I are not a couple. Really. We're just friends."

But even if we’re stuck in a big, slow double kayak for the day, Matt and I make the best of it. We paddle together in the sunshine through the sheltered waters of the inner islands, exploring deep, calm inlets and intertidal regions, watching as seals and seabirds float nearby.

“So, what’s the deal with the sailor?” Matt asks. “We’ve got all day. Spill.”

The thing about Matt is that I can tell him anything.

"We have an interesting dynamic," I start. I know this will draw Matt in. He loves dissecting relationships and exploring the dynamics at play between people.

"Yeah?"

"We have fun together. Lots to talk about. Lots of common interests."

"Right. He's the one who's done all the hiking and travelling."

"Yeah. Interesting guy. Loves the outdoors, loves travel, has amazing direction in his life."

"Uh oh. This sounds like more than a bit of summer fun."

"Nope." I'm decisive here. "We've got boundaries."

"Yeah?"

"He knows I'm not interested in being with him. And I know he's not interested in me. But we have fun together sailing."

"Careful..."

"He is so not the right guy for me. Trust me." I turn back in the kayak to look at Matt, wanting to reinforce the point. He does not look convinced.

"So here's the thing about the dynamics," I say. "When I'm not projecting into the future and imagining myself married to the guy, I can just accept him as he is."

"Finally! How many years have I been telling you this? This is why you have to be friends first."

"True. But he's still not the guy for me. If I were looking long-term, I would have bolted already." I paddle along for a bit. "It's interesting. There's no pressure. No expectation. And I feel like I can just be myself. I don't need to please him or impress him. It's amazingly liberating."

"And dangerous," Matt says. "Just keep those boundaries clear, my friend."

Matt and I enjoy ourselves that day in the double kayak, but we're both really happy to paddle the next day in singles. As we set out on our second day, I realize how much I love the sense of independence one has in a single kayak. I'm able to set my own pace, steer my own boat, and decide where I want to go and with whom I wanted to paddle. Looking over at Matt, a serene expression on his face, I realize he is equally happy.

Paddling over to him, I say, "I think the single kayak might be a metaphor for my life right now. I like being on my own, deciding where I want to go and what I want to do."

We laugh about how paddling a double is like being in a relationship. There's all that teamwork and compromise, and the petty irritations that arise between partners.

"Maybe I'm just supposed to be single for a while," I muse.

Except, of course, the rest of the group is still under the impression that we are an item. And our impromptu yoga session the next morning probably doesn't help.

I wake up in the tent, every muscle from my shoulders to my wrists aching. Matt, whom you might recall loves his yoga, sits up, still half in his sleeping bag, and starts stretching. I follow along, pushing my arms out in front of me, and then stretching them over my head, and then pulling them behind me.

"Oh! That feels so good," I groan.

It's weird how the rest of the group avoids eye contact with us at breakfast.

Late in August, Dan and I are out one evening on his boat. We're sharing a bottle of Malbec and watching the clouds swirl scarlet and gold as the sun sets. We've been talking about next steps in Dan's journey, and now he's turning my questions back on me. "And so, Sally, what's next for you?"

What's next? It's a question I'm feeling more ready to answer these days. I've spent the summer in a waiting period, letting go of my need to control the next stage of my life, and just enjoying the gifts of the moment. And in the process, I've started to find my way back to me. I'm beginning to recognize again what I value, and what I want and need in my life. And as I get clearer, I'm finding again my direction.

One of the hard truths I've had to face up to since Griff and I broke up is how easily I lose myself in a relationship. I don't do it purposefully, and I'm certainly not forced into it, but slowly I let go of what I want, and lose sight of what's important to me.

It's only when I'm single that I really stay focused on doing what's most important for me. And so what's next for me is a clear direction and then I need to make a commitment to myself not to compromise that direction before I enter into another long-term relationship.

I've often marvelled at the ways in which the universe delivers. When I wrote my first online dating profile, the summer after my divorce, I advertised for a man with "courage, brains and heart, someone with whom to take the first tentative steps on this new journey." I got exactly what I asked for, a lovely, healing summer fling that restored my faith in men and my belief in myself.

In the dating profile I wrote in May, I asked, "You know when you get to one of life's intersections and you're not quite sure where to head next? And you don't have a GPS? And the last copy of *The Lonely Planet's Guide to the Road Less Traveled* has been signed out at the library? I hate it when that happens. But here I am."

This is the profile with the playful tagline, "Easily Led Astray". But now, three months later, I'm shocked at how lost I sound. I haven't a clue what I want or need, and I haven't any sense of direction in my life.

And so it's interesting that *D is for Dan* has appeared in my life this summer, he with a purpose and a direction so clear that he actually has a compass tattooed on his calf.

And it's interesting that one of the things that he's been teaching me when we head out on his sailboat is how to chart a course and then steer in the right direction.

It's not easy, I've learned, to stay on course. There are winds and currents and all sorts of obstacles that pull a boat off course. In fact, I've become quite adept at steering the boat in perfect circles from time to time. But what Dan has shown me is that I need to keep my eyes on a fixed mark somewhere in the distance, and to just keep making regular, small adjustments to ensure that I stay on course. I'm getting better at it. Today I took the helm and kept us on course across a large, open channel. I didn't steer in circles once!

And so what's next for me? It's time to chart my own course, work out exactly what direction I'm headed in life, and then find a fixed mark from which to navigate. Only once I'm clear about my own direction can I entertain the possibility of entering another long-term relationship, and even then, I'll need to stay focused, making those small, regular adjustments to ensure that I stay on course.

It's time for me to take responsibility for my own direction, to own my inner compass, and to let go, once and for all, of the concept of easily led astray.

"So?" asks Kira, leaning toward me in the coffee shop. "How's the Man-batical going?"

I laugh. "It's the way to go, Sister! It has been so nice to get off those dating sites for the summer."

"It's exhausting to keep putting yourself out there," she sighs.

"You know what's been the best part? Just not having to decide. Just giving myself permission to not be looking. Just that has made me feel so much better."

Kira's nodding. She knows.

"And really, for me, it was the right thing. I did not need to blow through another ten dates and then politely tell them they weren't right for me. Especially when I had no idea what I was looking for."

"Do you have a better idea now?"

"Not really!" I laugh. "I don't think I'm quite ready to get back to dating."

Kira raises an eyebrow. "Don't tell me you're thinking about keeping Dan around."

I smile. "That was never the plan. For either of us. And really it's not like we spent the whole summer together. It was just a weekend here and there."

"On a sailboat."

I laugh again. “I know. It was probably a bit risky. But Dan and I are not meant to be together. It just worked to hang out together for a bit this summer.”

Kira gives me a long, quizzical look.

“Don’t worry! I’ll be back out there soon. I just can’t face it yet.”

# EIGHTEEN

# THE SLOW DATING MANIFESTO

The water tonight is like glass. The air is warm. It feels like the middle of August on the water, not the middle of September. Dan and I are out at Sidney Spit, enjoying one last free evening together, soaking up the late afternoon sunshine, and watching one more golden sunset.

The evening is bittersweet for me. The summer is over, a summer spent on the beach and on the water, a summer that has absolutely nurtured my mermaid heart. When I think back on the beach-side camping adventures with my boys, with my kayaking excursion with Matt, and with my sailing adventures with Dan, I realize I have had exactly the summer I needed, a beautiful, healing, happy stretch of time.

And so tonight, as the sun begins to drop over the island, I'm feeling a little sad. September for me means that my real-life schedule kicks in, a schedule filled with school pick-ups and play dates, soccer, dance and karate practices. And now that Dan is heading back to work, I know this is the last time we'll watch the sea and the sky slowly transform from the bright blues of the afternoon, to the pinks of evening, and into the blackness of night.

Tonight, I'm savouring every moment, committing to memory the tang of the salt air, the ripple of waves as a seal pokes its head up near the boat, the quality of light as dusk falls. I breathe in the warmth of the evening air, the stillness of the water, the quiet rock of the waves as one boat after another slowly leaves the spit and heads for home.

We linger late into the evening, waiting until night falls before firing up the motor, turning on the running lights, and making our way back toward the lights of Sidney. The sea is calm as we motor home, a deep, inky black, the sky bright with stars. It is utterly peaceful.

As we near home, Dan points to the wake streaming out behind the boat. In the blackness of the water, the wake glows bright with bioluminescence, the outer edges laced in a shimmering stream of pale green. It's a moment infused with the magic of this long, delicious summer.

Early the following morning, I'm in the grocery store, stocking up before the boys come back to me later in the day. As I'm choosing some apples for school lunches, an older man approaches me, holding a bunch of green onions, a tentative smile on his face. He has the sun-bleached, super-relaxed look of somebody who is still on vacation. "Excuse me," he starts. "Do you know how long green onions keep?"

I smile. "The green ends only last a couple of days, but if you cut those off, they'd last longer."

"I'm living on my sailboat for the summer," he says, and then offers an explanation that I hardly hear. I'm still focussed on the fact that this man is *living* on his sailboat. *For the whole summer.*

"Oh! You're so lucky," I gush. "I'd love to spend a whole summer on a sailboat! I was out at Sidney Spit last night. So beautiful."

"It is," he agrees, smiling. Then he holds up a bunch of radishes. "These would probably last on the boat, hey?"

We chat for a while about the merits of various vegetables on sailboats and then wander off towards different parts of the produce section. But he appears again as I'm picking up some potatoes. "So, do you sail with your husband?"

I smile at him. "No, just a friend who had space for me on his sailboat," I joke.

He looks at me speculatively. "Well," he grins, "if you'd like to come out sailing with me sometime..."

I laugh. "Now that is a very tempting offer." I'm enjoying myself. I love a little bit of harmless flirting in the grocery store. Picking up my grocery basket, I wave to him. "Enjoy these last beautiful weeks of summer out on your boat!"

He smiles and waves back.

A few minutes later, when I'm at the deli counter, my sailor from the produce section approaches me again. He looks apologetic. "I'm sorry to bother you again," he starts. "But I'm curious. How did you meet your sailing friend?"

I give him a sheepish grin and confess. "Actually, I met him on a dating site. I didn't want to date him, but we became friends. And this summer we were both single and both had a few free weekends..." I trail off, wondering why I'm sharing this information.

My new friend thanks me. "Maybe I should try that," he says. "I'd love to find someone to sail with."

"I'll bet there are all kinds of women out there who would love the opportunity," I tell him. I give him another warm smile as I head off to pick up the last of my groceries.

I'm in the checkout line when he approaches again. "So, one last question."

I laugh. "Okay!"

"What was it about your friend that first interested you? Why did you agree to meet him in the first place?"

I think back to Dan's profile. "I liked his sense of adventure. He sailed. He'd travelled. He was into the outdoors."

The man is nodding thoughtfully.

"And he'd climbed Mt. Kilimanjaro, which I thought was pretty cool."

The man's eyes widen. "I've climbed Kili!"

"Really?"

"Yes, and I've climbed Mt. Kenya too, which is a much more technical climb." He looks triumphant. "Are you sure you don't need a new sailing partner?"

I smile. "I would love that. But real life and all that." I wave a hand over the big pile of groceries. "Kids. Work."

He's nodding thoughtfully.

As I pay for my groceries, I turn to him and add, "I think there's an adventurous woman out there just waiting for you, one with the time to spend her whole summer sailing with you."

I feel myself smiling all the way home, uplifted by the interchange with my grocery store sailor. It's only later that night that I realize that this exchange was a little sign for me from the universe.

*Hey,* the universe is whispering. *Look at you. All relaxed and happy and whole. You're attracting men to you again. Maybe you're ready now.*

In late September, I wake one morning to the haunting moan of a foghorn. More than the chill in the morning air or the maples dropping their russet leaves, the sound of a fog horn signals the change of seasons for me. Every fall, the fog rolls in overnight and hangs low over the sea and in the fields until the autumn sun burns it away. I love waking to the foghorns, love listening to their deep call as I lie warm in my bed. But they remind me, too, that summer is behind us, that it's time to dig out the sweaters and boots, and prepare for a colder, rainier season. Loathe as I am to bid goodbye to summer, fall is a time of renewal for me.

Having spent years as a classroom teacher, I've come to associate autumn with new beginnings. And this fall is no different. I had a lovely summer spent on the water and on the beach, sailing and camping and kayaking. I was truly in my element. There was time to enjoy my kids, time with friends, time for sailing and kayaking. And some time, I spent, very happily, on my own. It was a summer spent far from Internet dating sites, far removed from the pressures of finding a new relationship. I feel rejuvenated by the break. I feel as though my heart, bruised after Griff, has healed.

But as October approaches, I realize that I really don't want to throw myself back into the treacherous seas of online dating.

"I'm feeling so good," I tell Linda the next time I'm in her office. "I'm in this happy, centered, calm place. I don't know if I can put myself through all that craziness again."

She smiles that maddening therapist smile. "Why are you so centered, do you think?"

"Because I'm not on *Plenty of Fish*, of course." I'm hoping for a laugh, but Linda just smiles expectantly and waits for me to go on.

"I guess it's probably because I took such good care of myself this summer?" She nods, waiting for more. Sighing, I continue. "I did all the things I know I should do to look after myself."

"Like?"

"Writing. Exercising. Eating well."

She nods and waits.

"Spending time with friends. Hanging out with the kids. Sailing. Kayaking."

"You did all the things you love to do."

"Yeah." I smile as I think of my perfect summer. "It was a bit indulgent really."

"Not really. Look at how you're feeling now. Calm. Centered. That's because you spent your summer filling your own tank. That's not indulgent. It isn't selfish. Think of it as being self-full."

I nod, a little skeptically. "I feel really good right now."

"And you want to hold on to that feeling. Going forward you need to look after yourself just as carefully."

"And stay off the Internet," I joke.

She gazes at me for a moment and then speaks. "It seems to me that you might be in the kind of healthy place you need to be to get back on the Internet. You might be ready to meet somebody now."

I let Linda's words sink in, hearing the truth of them.

Driving home after my appointment, I think back to the last time I felt this good, this whole. It was on my first-ever solo vacation, a year and a half after my divorce.

I remember wandering down narrow stone streets, past bright, whitewashed buildings, past doors painted in shades of creamy blue, past intricate iron gates. The evening sun was still warm. The sea, when I glimpsed it, flashed turquoise and silver. I was on Santorini, exploring the Greek island by myself. It was the first time in my life that I'd traveled alone. And I was perfectly content and at ease.

It's a few years now since that trip to Greece, but that experience for me was pivotal. Santorini has become for me a touchstone, a reminder when I begin to feel uncomfortable with being alone. When I think back to my time on Santorini, I remember the freedom and the spaciousness of my alone-ness; the leisurely meals, eaten in tiny restaurants overlooking the sea. I remember lingering in those restaurants, sipping a cold glass of white wine and watching the sun begin to set. Sometimes, I'd write. Sometimes, I'd just sit and breathe in the experience of solitude.

I'd lose myself in the labyrinth of streets, wandering with no greater purpose than to really see the place, delighting in the discovery of another whitewashed home with a brightly painted door, another glimpse of the sparkling sea, another perfect vista. I'd rise with the sun, and head out to take photographs in the warm early morning light. I kept thinking, *I feel so content, so happy. This is what it feels like to be alone.*

After this lovely summer, I'm in that happy, centered, content place again. It's the place I needed to get to after the end of my relationship with Griff. It's been a long journey, the better part of a year now. But these days I feel balanced and healthy, content in my life exactly as it is.

Does it mean that I want to be alone long term? Not at all. I love being in a relationship, I love sharing my life with a man, I love all that good stuff. I'd like nothing more than to find the right guy. I know it will happen, and more and more, I feel ready for it to happen. But I feel no rush, no sense of panic.

I remember the last morning of my stay on Santorini. I trod hundreds of stone stairs down to the beach. It was early in the morning and there was nobody else around. The buildings were bathed in soft early light and the sea sparkled a thousand shades of green and blue. At the bottom of the stairs, I found an outdoor cafe, deserted because of the hour. Pulled up onto the patio, beside a table, was a solitary boat. It was battered and its paint had worn away. This boat had seen storms. But as I came closer, I saw that it still had oars tucked inside, and nets for fishing. This little boat, I realized, was just biding its time until the tide was right. And then it would head out to sea once more.

It isn't just Linda who shares her wisdom at this time. It is in the in-between time when I'm beginning to contemplate dating again that I also seek out the palm reader in the shopping mall. So much of what she tells me that day rings true, though in fairness she doesn't get everything right. For example, she is sure that I have perfect pitch. I most assuredly do not.

And she's convinced that I'll be heading off to Australia in the near future. Australia doesn't even make my *Top Ten List* for places I'd like to see. Besides, they have big, poisonous spiders there. It's a place I can happily give a miss. Forever.

It's the palm reader's final observations that stay with me. "You have a childlike heart," she tells me. "You see the good in the world, the wonder. There is no bitterness or pessimism. But your heart is about five years old. You have to protect it."

That's certainly what I've been doing this last year, discarding any man who might be remotely capable of breaking my heart, and holding the rest at a safe, manageable distance. I am skilled, I realize, at protecting my heart.

As I'm leaving, she says, "The really important question you need to ask yourself about any man is whether he is somebody who will protect you, no matter what." In the days that follow, her words echo, until I'm left with a single phrase, a question to ask myself about any man I go out with: "Can he protect my heart?"

A little reluctantly, I start working on a new profile. It's time to ditch "Easily Led Astray." It's time to delete all those references to being lost and without direction. I know what I want.

I just don't really believe that I can have it.

When my marriage ended, the thing I was most upset about was losing my sense of family. Family was the thing I'd invested most heavily in and when my ex-husband left me, I felt like he destroyed our family in the process. It took me a long while to forgive him and to understand that family is a word with many definitions. In the years since the divorce, I've created a new sense of family for my boys, a stable, loving home with just the four of us. If there's one thing I know, it's that I'm a good mom.

And what I really want, when I have the courage to admit it, is a man who adores me, who protects my heart, and who has an adventurer's soul. All that. And also I want that man to be someone with whom I could create another, updated definition for family. I don't want to keep my family life and my romantic life separate any longer.

It's only Linda who believes this is possible. "You can have it all, Sally," she tells me.

And so I write a new profile, one that lays it all out, that says who I really am, with all my contradictions.

*I believe in laughter and curiosity and good conversation; in kindness and honesty and trust; in warmth and affection.*

*I believe in the value of deep and abiding friendships; in the importance of family and community; I believe there are few things better than sitting around a dinner table with good friends and laughing late into the night.*

*I believe in seizing the day and in taking risks. I believe in giving my free spirit free rein and in seeking adventures big and small. I believe in seeing the world.*

*And despite all evidence to the contrary, I still believe in happily ever after.*

*Enough about me.... You are strong and intelligent, open-minded and playful. You are grounded, but have an adventurous soul. Beyond that, I'll trust in serendipity...*

*I finish with a new tagline: "Heading in my direction?"*

It's just as I'm getting up the courage to launch the new profile that one of my co-workers approaches me with a proposal.

"Hey, Sally. Did you see today's Groupon for speed dating? Jess and I are going. Why don't you come too?" Allie has a wicked gleam in her eye. I'm not sure whether she's serious or not.

She's serious.

"Come on, it'll be fun! We'll go for a drink first, then go speed dating, and then have a drink together after and compare notes."

She's serious. But she's laughing too. "This could be a good laugh," she says. "So what did you think about number eight? Do you think that was his real hair? It'll be fun!"

But I don't see anything funny about it. In fact the very thought of speed dating makes me feel queasy. I can't imagine anything worse than sitting at a table and having a series of men circulate past, giving me the five minute version of themselves. The whole idea of speed dating wigs me out. It's ironic really, considering how many first dates I've gone on in the last five years.

I'll admit that I'm torn. On the one hand, my negative reaction to speed dating is visceral.

On the other hand, it would make for a great blog post

But I can't do it. Not even for the laugh.

I'm trying to figure out what it is about the concept of speed dating that makes me feel nauseous. And I realize that it's because I was engaged in my own version of speed dating in the spring. I've done the calculations. *A is for Adam* to *S is for Stefan* equals nineteen first dates. Nineteen dates in four months. *The Alphabet Dating Game* might have seemed like a good blog concept, but it was a terrible idea for my love life.

So instead of speed dating, I'm embracing a new approach. I've always liked the idea of the slow food movement, and so I'm going to impose upon myself a similar approach to dating. I am going to start a slow dating movement!

And what does this mean for me? It means I will only date local men. No long distance, no matter how appealing. It means I will not panic and open up my profile when I'm only communicating with one or two men. I do not need to have a number of men in the wings just in case. Repeat after me: I do not need backup men. I do not need backup men. It means I will stay open in the dating process and will be honest and forthright in my interactions. I will not dump a man after one date for trivial reasons. I will remain open-minded. And I will avoid placing expectations or pressure on an emerging relationship. I will stay in the moment!

I'm excited about this new approach. I think it's healthy. I think it's sane. I think it's a way for me get to know people the way I got to know Dan during the summer.

And besides, I need to slow down. I only have seven letters left in the alphabet.

# NINETEEN

# THE MEN OF OCTOBER

The last sun of an October afternoon slants across the patio, lighting the beers on the table and warming my hands and face. I'm having a beer with Tom, my first date in more than three months. Tom is a tall, fit man, with a weathered face. He's expressive and funny, and a great conversationalist. As I sit across from him, I realize that I'm feeling relaxed and comfortable: I'm enjoying myself. I can't say that I'm feeling any real chemistry, but I'm having fun. And maybe for now, that's enough. Maybe if I stay open, the chemistry will come.

In keeping with my slow dating manifesto, I've kept my profile hidden and mostly stayed off *Plenty of Fish*. I spent an evening completing a search for professional men with children in my age range. Among them, Tom seemed the most attractive option, and after a couple of emails back and forth we decided to meet for a walk along the Victoria waterfront. The walk has morphed into a late afternoon beer, and the conversation continues to flow.

"So then they moved me into statement analysis," he says, telling me more about the years he spent in law enforcement. "They actually sent me off for training with a former member of Mossad."

"I've never heard of statement analysis."

"When you're trained in statement analysis, you can look at a piece of writing and identify where a person is lying."

I gulp. "A piece of writing like a dating profile, for example?"

He laughs. "Hmmm. I hadn't thought about it, but it's not a bad idea! Maybe I'll analyze yours for you."

Now it's my turn to laugh. I hope it comes off as light-hearted.

And not panicked.

For a woman like me, who spends half her free time blogging and the other half Internet dating, statement analysis is a terrifying concept. As Tom tells me more about how one analyses a document, I'm doing a quick mental scan of what I've written.

Hopefully he'll understand that when I say I like adventure, that I mean "small a" adventure. You're not going to find me ice climbing a frozen waterfall or leaping out of a small plane with nothing more than a flimsy little parachute that might or might not work.

Hopefully he'll understand that when I say I like to keep active, that what I mean is that I really love to buy cute workout gear and so occasionally feel the need to justify the purchase by dragging my ass to a class or to the gym.

It's not that I'm lying about anything, but I'm not telling the whole truth either.

Tom relates a story about the documents a suspected murderer had written, and my mind wanders further.

I realize that even though I know my own profile isn't entirely honest, *I believe everything men say in their profiles!*

I read, "I'm a glass half full kind of guy," and think, *great! I love positive people!*

A man writes, "I would do anything for you," and I think, *he sounds so nice!*

It's clear that I would make a terrible police officer and it's also clear that maybe I shouldn't take those profiles at face value. I might agree, for example, to date a man who says he's retired. But retired and unemployed aren't quite the same thing.

The trouble with the truth is that it isn't always attractive. By the time we hit our forties, we're all hauling baggage. Loads of it. We have ex-wives and husbands. Old boyfriends and girlfriends. Badly behaved children. We've been around long enough to have more than a few skeletons in our closets. You would not believe some of the stories I've heard.

Even if we're totally together in our personal lives, our eyesight is failing. Our joints might be giving us trouble. The women are heading toward menopause. Some of the men are beginning to appreciate the virtues of Viagra. Our medicine cabinets are full. Women like me have come to rely on regular visits to the colorist, because heaven knows that there will be no dates if we let ourselves go grey.

The whole truth is simply not an option. We'd never get a date again.

"Hey," Tom says, interrupting my reverie. "This was fun. Do you want to get together again some time?"

Tom and I meet a couple more times, and each time the conversation is lively. But though we can easily talk and laugh away an afternoon, there just doesn't seem to be any chemistry between us. And I don't think it's just me feeling that way. I can tell that Tom enjoys hanging out with me, but he too seems quite happy to keep things at the level of hugs and high fives.

I've made a commitment to take things slowly and to not judge too quickly, and so I'm prepared to see what unfolds. But after three dates, it's Tom who calls things off, sending me a graceful note admitting that he's just not feeling the chemistry between us.

I send him an email back that would hold up against even the most rigorous statement analysis.

*Dear Tom,*

*It has been really fun getting to know you over the last couple of weeks. There seems to be lots of good energy between us and we certainly know how to have a good laugh together. But, like you, I'm not feeling that spark.*

*Nevertheless, I'm glad to have met you, and glad that we got to spend that perfect autumn afternoon together in East Sooke Park. May the perfect woman appear soon in your life!*

*Sally*

After Tom, I find myself in a funny place as far as dating goes, hardly able to conjure the energy to communicate with anyone, let alone to actually set up a face-to-face meeting.

Perhaps it's because I am so perilously close to the end of the alphabet. Perhaps I'm happy enough on my own. Perhaps I'm just not that interested.

I complete half-hearted searches, looking for possible matches, but once I narrow the search to men who are educated, employed and family oriented, there are very few options. As I scan the possibilities, I see the faces of men I've dated before and of men I've ruled out before; beyond that, the pickings, as they say, are slim.

Interested in not even one of the possible matches, I decide to open up my profile. I remind myself that there are men who are doing the same as I am, who are keeping their profiles hidden and completing the same demoralizing searches. We're never going to find each other if we've both got hidden profiles.

If I only open my profile up for a single evening, I tell myself, I can maintain a modicum of control over things. Feeling shaky, but still hopeful, I open my profile on a Friday and then head out with friends.

By Saturday morning, there is a pile of new email in my *Plenty of Fish* inbox, and before I even open it, I hide my profile again. *Take it slow*, I remind myself. *Stay open to the possibilities in your inbox, Sally.*

In fact the possibilities are limited. But I'm intrigued by the profile of one man, who writes about his recent travels in Italy and whose pictures feature him in various spots in the Tuscan countryside. His children are grown, and he seems to be nearing retirement, both points that concern me. But I remind myself that I've been completely open about how important and how young my boys are. Surely he'll have read my profile.

You know what they say about assuming things?

As we sip coffee together, Umberto stretches out his long legs and runs his fingers through tousled graying curls. He has a rumpled look about him, as though he's slept in his clothes. In a quiet voice, he tells me about his travels in Italy and his plans to return. He's looking for somebody, he tells me, who would also like to travel, and eventually relocate, to Italy.

When I bring up my children, he seems genuinely surprised.

*Hello Umberto,*

*It was lovely to meet you yesterday and to hear all about your recent adventures in Tuscany and it left me longing to return to that part of the world.*

*I can't see things working out for us, Umberto. But I have a suspicion that perhaps you're meant to return once more to Tuscany. Perhaps the girl you're meant to meet is waiting for you already in Italy.*

*Sally*

"I'm considering the convent," I tell Kira over coffee a week later. "I can't do this anymore!"

She clucks sympathetically.

"You should have seen the guy I met for coffee yesterday," I start. "As soon as he walked through the door, I knew I'd made a mistake. I've never seen anyone so overdue for a haircut. He looked a little like Bozo the Clown. And his fingernails." I grimace at the thought. "They really needed cutting."

Kira is giggling already.

"He bought me a coffee and bought himself an orange pop!"

The giggles turn to hoots.

"And then he started telling me about the blow up cat that he drives around with."

Loud guffaws. The other people in the coffee shop are turning to look at us now.

"Why did you go out with him in the first place?" Kira asks.

"He was a good writer," I say miserably. "I am such a sucker for a funny email."

Kira nods. She's been there.

"There was so much that was *just wrong* about him! In his profile he talked about all the countries he's visited. Turns out most of his traveling happened with his parents. When he was a child. And he's unemployed! Small detail."

Hoots of laughter once again.

"Easy for you, my friend," I laugh. "Safely removed from the dating websites. How is the captain of the football team?"

Kira has recently started a relationship with a fun-loving man who spoils her rotten. She loves to remind me that her new beau is much younger than she is and was an all-star athlete in high school. "Finally!" she crows. "Finally, I'm dating the captain of the football team!"

"He's good." She smiles dreamily. "And he never orders orange pop."

*Hi Vern,*

*It was nice to meet you yesterday but I can't see things working out for us. It seems like you are in a real place of transition in your life right now and my sense is that you probably need to focus on that transition first. I wish you much luck in your search for a rewarding new career and in your search for the right girl.*

*Sally*

It's a cold afternoon near the end of October and Matt and I are walking fast along the waterfront through rain and wind. We've caught up about family and work and I'm filling him in on my recent dating misadventures. "You know, I really felt like I was going to get it right after the summer," I start. "But now I'm attracting men with blow up cats!"

Matt laughs. "You do seem in a good place, all calm and balanced." He gives me a sideways grin. "Yep. Way less hysterical than usual."

"Thanks," I laugh. "Do you remember right after Griff and I broke up you asked me what I wasn't giving myself? What I was waiting for a man to give me? Turns out it was a pretty long list."

Matt raises an eyebrow. "Really?"

"Yeah, and it goes way beyond taking care of myself."

"You're pretty good at that. You've been doing it long enough."

"Yeah. I've got the single mother thing figured out. It's not like I need somebody to look after me. But all spring I kept going out with world travellers and adventurers who would never fit into my life. And what I finally realized was that I wasn't giving myself any adventures."

"So the Broken Islands."

"And camping and sailing. New Orleans next week."

"Nice." Matt is smiling, like I've finally figured out something that is blindingly obvious to everyone else.

"And," I add, "I'm even figuring out my addiction to alpha males."

Matt slows down and looks at me. "Yeah?"

"Maybe I need to own that ambition in myself."

Matt nods. "Makes sense."

"I know. And I'd just like to say that with all this hard won wisdom, I should have found a guy by now."

New Orleans in late October is humid and summertime-warm. My friend Kim and I are here with our colleague Jane in order to attend a conference, and we've added a few extra days to the trip to explore the city. In preparation, Jane has been visualizing a meeting with Harry Connick Jr. "I just know we're going to see him," Jane tells us in the departures lounge at the airport. "New Orleans is Harry's home town. It's going to happen."

Every morning, Jane enlists our help. "Work with me, girls," she starts. "Close your eyes and imagine Harry walking down the street toward us."

"I don't think I even know what he looks like!"

"Then just repeat this mantra: Harry Connick Jr. Harry Connick Jr."

Kim laughs. "Sally, maybe you should try this approach instead of *Plenty of Fish!*"

"I have been, but so far no luck."

"Maybe you need to be more specific."

I laugh. "Tall, dark and handsome," I try. "Tall, dark and handsome." But it's a half-hearted attempt.

On our last day in New Orleans, as we're wandering through the French Quarter, we hear music playing. Following the sound, we round a corner, and there, in the middle of the street, flanked by camera crews and equipment, is Harry Connick Jr. He's dancing, snapping his fingers and singing, "You are my Sunshine."

Jane beams at us. "Told you," she says as I squeeze in beside her to watch.

And as Harry does his thing, singing and dancing, occasionally turning to play a few notes on the piano behind him, I wonder when I lost my faith in the universe. When did I lose faith that I could find that one good man?

But the universe, when I listen, keeps whispering to me. It's while we're in New Orleans that I'm reminded again that I'm ready to meet someone. While Kim and Jane spend a day shopping, I head off on a swamp tour, and spend my day meeting new people, including a number of men.

That evening, as Jane, Kim and I wander down Frenchman Street, I bump into one after another of these people.

"Jim! Hello again," I say, as I run into my new friend from California. "This must be your daughter?"

Kim and Jane are curious. "How did you meet him?"

"We were on the swamp tour together."

And what about that couple you were talking to outside the bar?"

"They're staying at the same hotel as we are. I grabbed a cab with them."

A muscular Jamaican man walks towards us and holds out his arms to hug me.

"Oh. My. God!" Kim exclaims. Do you know everyone here?"

I don't. But I've spent my day on my own, so have interacted with loads of people over the course of the day. And it seems that every person I've had a conversation with is down here tonight on Frenchman Street.

It's the universe again. I'm sure of it. *You're ready, Sally. You're open and happy and full of life. You're ready now to meet somebody.*

# TWENTY

## W IS FOR WILL

After the little break in New Orleans, I decide to follow Jane's example. A bit of visualization and a mantra can't hurt. It brought Jane her encounter with Harry. I delve back into my journal and read over the things I'm looking for in a partner. There they are, on a dog-eared page, each trait circled and underlined: I'm looking for chemistry, kindness, and intelligence; I'm looking for someone who is responsible, but also light-hearted and adventurous; I want somebody who is ready for commitment. *One good man*, I think.

It's the Sunday night of a long weekend and I'm at loose ends, and so late in the evening, I open my profile for another evening and see what happens. I've uploaded some new pictures, including one of Kim, Jane and me on Bourbon Street. Nobody can accuse me of using outdated photos. *One good man*, I whisper to myself. *One good man.*

A couple of hours later, I check my *Plenty of Fish* account. Sure enough, there are a number of new messages, and idly I go through them. A number of nos. A couple of maybes. One guy who doesn't even have a profile picture. I'm always a bit suspicious about men who don't post pictures, but I open the message anyway. "If not gelato on the Spanish Steps, perhaps an afternoon at the Prado?" The message is signed by somebody called Will. Hmm. He's obviously read all the way through my profile to the section where I've suggested gelato in Rome as a first date. And he knows what the Prado is.

It's enough to get me to open his profile, which is funny and self-deprecating. "I won't tell you that I have a six pack," it reads. "That would be a fib. The only six pack around here is in my fridge." He writes well, revealing that he is Australian, has a son to whom he is devoted, and that he's a professional. It's enough for me to send a response.

"I've always been more partial to Italy than to Spain. Gelato first and then the Prado?"

I return to the other messages in my account and begin crafting a couple of "Thanks but no thanks" messages. But almost instantly, another email from Will appears. I'm surprised. Most men don't respond right away. I like it when a man dispenses with the games that are so much a part of the online dating culture.

"And after Italy and Spain," Will writes, "perhaps a side trip to Morocco?" I smile. Here's someone who knows how to play to my adventurous side. "I've attached a photo," he adds. "Sorry it's not very good. My son took it!"

I look at the photo, which is truly terrible. It's blurry and tilted, clearly the work of a child. Will is standing in a back yard, mostly in shadow, and all I can really see is that he's stocky and balding. It would be hard to draw any conclusions about the man from a photo this bad. I'm having fun with the emails, though, so I reply.

"I've always wanted to go to Morocco. What do you suggest we do there?" And thus begins a playful set of emails back and forth planning an imaginary adventure together.

After we've planned our trip, Will writes, "I think I recognize one of your friends in the picture on Bourbon Street. Is that Kim Andrews?"

I'm taken aback. "How do you know Kim?"

"I taught with her when I first came to Canada on teacher exchange."

I feel my heart sink. He's a teacher. In all my time dating, I have studiously avoided teachers. In the nearly fifty first dates I've been out on, I haven't once dated a teacher. There is no greater turn off for me than seeing a man's school photo as his profile picture. It's irrational, I know. Though I'm no longer a classroom teacher, I still work in the world of education. Going out with a teacher would make perfect sense. But my ex-husband was a teacher when I first met him and I don't want to go down that particular road again.

*Stay open,* I tell myself, and respond. "Kim is one of my dearest friends. Small world, hey?"

"Any chance you'd be available for a coffee tomorrow?" Will writes. "I know it's short notice."

Despite his teacher status, I've enjoyed our exchange and say yes. "Actually, tomorrow works. My kids are with their dad right now, so I have some free time."

I'm heading toward the coffee shop we've planned to meet at, when I see Will from across the road. He's shorter than the men I usually date, but even in his bulky winter coat, I can see that he's muscular. He recognizes me, waves, and crosses over to my side. "Hello," he says, his voice warm, his Australian accent soft. I smile, taking in brown eyes and cinnamon-coloured skin. There's something about him that I'm drawn to immediately. We stand a little awkwardly, in that moment when neither a handshake nor a hug is the right option. Will gestures toward the coffee shop. "Can I buy you a drink?"

I always dread the first few minutes of a coffee date, before the conversation really starts. We're standing in line, smiling at each other, but not sure where to start.

"So you worked with Kim, hey?" I start.

"I did. We worked in the same department the year I was here on exchange."

"It's funny," I say. "I don't remember hearing about you."

He laughs, a deep, rich laugh that I like right away "I'm not sure what she thought of me. It was a bit of a party year for me." He offers a self-deprecating grin. "I spent more time in the pubs that first year in Canada than I have in the ten years since."

We head back out into the November cold, and as we walk, Will tells me a little about how he came to stay in Victoria, how he fell in love, and in his forties decided to emigrate from Australia to Canada.

I look at him in wonder. "I can't imagine ever taking a leap like that."

He shrugs. "It was what I wanted."

I'm quiet for a moment, processing the story. "And it didn't work out," I say quietly, feeling sad for him.

"I have my little bloke," he says, his voice softening. "That's all that matters."

"What's his name?"

"Simon. He's such a beautiful little boy. The best thing that's ever happened to me." I can hear the obvious love in Will's voice and am surprised by how much it touches me.

Will and I sit on the beach, watching the waves fly in, grey and cold as the November day. We've walked a long way, and shared stories about our respective histories and our families. We discover that we share quite a bit in common, even if I've lived most of my life in Canada and Will in Australia. We've both recently lost a parent, and as Will talks about his mum, his voice chokes. I know that feeling. It happens every time I talk about my dad. In fact Will reminds me of Dad, with his warmth and his wry sense of humour. I'm surprised by how comfortable I feel just sitting with this man I've only just met. I listen to his soft Australian accent and think, *I like you.*

I know already that I'll go out with him again.

"Hey!" I lean into Kim's office the next day at work. "I went out for coffee with someone you know yesterday."

"You did? Who?"

I'm almost afraid to say his name. I like Will and want to see him again. "Your Aussie friend, Will."

"Will?" Kim's face breaks into a big grin. "I love that man!" She goes on to tell me what a good teacher he was and how much fun it was to have him on staff. "We've never had a better year-end party than the one that Will helped organize," she says laughing. "Those were some good margaritas!" Then she looks at me carefully. "He's a good guy, Sally."

"Yeah. I thought so too."

About a week later, Will and I get together again to walk a long, lakeside trail. Like me, he has a degree in literature, and we've been discussing our favourite authors. "I haven't read many Canadians writers," Will tells me. "I love Ondaatje, though," he says, "and Rohinton Mistry. Have you read their work?"

I laugh, remembering that in the long list of qualities I compiled back in February, I'd actually written, "I'd like a man who's read Rohinton Mistry." As Will talks about other writers I'm not as familiar with, I notice how articulate he is, how intelligent. It's funny, because he's told me all about his years playing cricket, a game I know nothing about, and about his passion for rugby, baseball and golf, and so I've already categorized him as a jock. But as he talks about Salman Rushdie's work, I realize I've underestimated this man. Time passes quickly as we discuss literature and then travel. I'm entranced by Will's stories of his travels through Asia. It's a part of the world I'm longing to visit.

We've walked nearly the entire perimeter of the lake when talk turns to our experiences on dating sites, a topic that inevitably comes up if a date is long enough. "So how long have you been on *Plenty of Fish*," I ask.

"Off and on over the last few years," Will says.

"Did you meet anyone there?" I ask, my curiosity overcoming my manners.

"No," Will says, looking ahead on the trail. "I wasn't really looking for someone. I wasn't in the right frame of mind." A long silence. "After Mum died last summer, I decided I didn't want to be on my own for the rest of my life."

"So you haven't had a relationship since your divorce?"

"No."

"And you've been divorced seven years?" I'm trying not to sound incredulous.

Will shrugs. "It took me a long time to get over things," he says quietly.

Will walks me back to my car and in that awkward moment as the date ends, he smiles and says, "Can I kiss you?" I laugh, knowing he's referring to the No Kissing policy in my dating profile. I lean towards him and he gives me a brief kiss. It's the first kiss I've welcomed in months.

*Dear Will,*

*You asked me last night if I believe in fate. When I think of fate, I think of predetermination, of an outcome that is fixed and over which I have no control. I think that we end up where we do because of choices. So no, I don't believe in fate.*

*But I do believe in serendipity, in the happy accidents that sometimes shape our lives. You found me on Plenty of Fish in one of those rare windows when I opened my profile.*

*I don't believe in fate. But I do believe in good timing. If you'd found me six months ago, I wouldn't have been ready for you. Your open, forthright approach would have scared the hell out of me. Five minutes and I'd have been running for the hills.*

*I don't believe in fate. But I do believe in "bloody good luck." What are the chances of meeting somebody with whom you feel an instant connection, an instant sense of comfort?*

*There's so much I like about you, Will. You're warm and kind and funny. You're intelligent and responsible. You love the same Indian writers that I do. And you've got just enough of the rebel Australian bad boy in you to give you an edge. I like you, Will. And I really like your delicious Aussie accent.*

*Here's to serendipity, Will, to good timing and to a bit of "bloody good luck."*

*Let's see what happens next.*

*Sally*

# TWENTY-ONE

# AT THE EDGE

Will and I start seeing each other regularly, though our respective parenting responsibilities prevent us from spending a great deal of time together. We're out together for a Tuesday night beer and talking about how lucky we'd been to find each other on *Plenty of Fish*, given that both of us had been keeping our profiles hidden.

"What if the Cubs had been playing the night I opened my profile?" I tease him. "We'd never have met."

"If the Cubs had been playing, you'd have been out of luck," he says, his eyes twinkling. "A man has to have priorities." But then he smiles at me. "We'd have met. We were meant to meet."

I smile back. "I don't know. If you hadn't found me that night, I might still be out there trolling the Internet, pulling up one unsuitable catch after another."

"No, we would have met. It would have happened somehow."

"I hope so. Or else I'd still be politely turning down Sexy Cougar Hunter and Phil McCracken."

"Phil McCracken?" Will is laughing.

"No lie. There really was a Phil McCracken on *eHarmony*. I was matched up with him in my first week there."

Will is laughing so hard he's nearly in tears.

"I know, right? I mean what kind of idiot would actually expect a woman to respond to a name like that?"

Will catches his breath and then starts laughing again. "That was me," he gasps. "I was Phil McCracken!"

I'm stunned into silence.

But only for a moment. "I can't believe you! Why would you choose a name like that?"

"I was being an ass," Will says, still laughing. "I just wanted to check out the site. I didn't want anyone to actually contact me."

I'm shaking my head at him. "How old are you again? Fourteen?"

"Don't you think this is funny? You're actually out having a beer with Phil McCracken!"

I'm not seeing the humour in the situation. Sensing this, Will puts his arm around me and pulls me toward him. "You're a bit precious, you are," he says. "But I like you anyway."

I smile. "I like you too. Even if you're an idiot sometimes."

He laughs again. "You're a bloody beauty" And he gives me a kiss.

I wander into Will's kitchen one Saturday morning, still sleepy.

"Good morning, " he says, gathering me in for a hug and a kiss. After a long moment, he looks at me and says, "You looked so beautiful last night. I was so proud to be with you."

I feel my heart open. We'd been at his staff Christmas party, the first time we'd been out together as a couple. I'd been really nervous about the event, but I needn't have been. Throughout the evening, his friends and colleagues had gone out of their way to make me feel welcome. One woman approached me, and looking over at Will, said, "I adore that man." She told me about how Will had seen her husband through a difficult time in his life. Looking at me meaningfully, she added, "You need to know that Will has a heart of gold."

Will releases me from our hug and asks, "Would you like some coffee?"

"If you're having some."

"I can't drink it any more, but I made some for you." He pours me a mug of coffee. "Sit down," he says. "I'm just making breakfast."

I watch as he toasts croissants, drapes them with smoked salmon, and tops them with slowly scrambled eggs.

"This is divine," I say after my first bite.

He leans over and kisses me. “I’m not a bad cook, you know.”

Perhaps a month after I start seeing Will, I’m in Starbucks one morning, catching up on some of my favourite blogs, when *T is for Tom* walks in.

"Hey you!" he says, smiling broadly as he comes over and plunks himself into the chair beside me. "Who are you writing about today?"

"Tom! Nice to see you! I'm reading blogs right now, not writing."

After a pause, I add, "And I think maybe I've met someone."

"That's great!" he says. We talk for a couple of minutes about Will, and then Tom leans in and says, "I've met someone too. In fact, we just bought a house together."

"What? Are you serious?"

Tom laughs at my reaction and nods.

"But you and I went out together a couple of times in October! That’s not even two months ago! How long have you known this woman?"

"We met in the summer," he tells me. "And we really liked each other. But it was so intense that we both got scared off and ran away."

"And now you've bought a house together? I can't believe you!"

Tom laughs at me. "You know what? She's perfect for me. I call her my evil twin. Since I got past my fear, it's been great."

I'm still shaking my head in amazement, but I can see how happy he looks. "You're crazy, man. But in a good way."

He shrugs. "I'm fifty-two. I'm not going to let fear stand in the way of happiness. I see too many people living like that, living from a place of fear or mistrust."

I can't see myself leaping with Tom's abandon, but I admire his fearlessness. I've seen first hand what fear looks like in the dating world, how easy it is to live in a place without trust. There are so many ways that we protect ourselves from the possibility of further hurt

It takes enormous courage to put our past hurts and betrayals behind us, and allow ourselves to be open and vulnerable, to risk the possibility of heartbreak. But unless we open ourselves, we miss out on the possibility, and the pleasure of love.

Tom appears at exactly the right time for me, just as I'm getting to know somebody new who has the potential of a long term partner. I know my patterns. I know that when things start getting serious, I panic, push away, run.

It's time for me to adopt a little bit of Tom's courage. It's time for me to risk a little. I might not be ready to leap from the cliff, the way Tom has, but perhaps I can at least take a peek over the edge.

Tom's example gives me the courage to introduce Will to my boys. For me, this is a huge step. Since the divorce, I have kept my romantic life and my family life almost completely separate, going out on dates only when my boys are with their dad and not involving my kids at all. The only man the boys have gotten to know is Griff, but even with him, I was very cautious, waiting months to introduce him, and granting him very limited access to the boys throughout our relationship.

"How about if I pick you up tonight?" Will suggests when he and I are planning to go out together for a beer one night. The boys are with me, and my plan is to get the two youngest to bed and leave David, who's fifteen, in charge for a couple of hours. Having Will pick me up at the house is definitely not part of my plan. But for some reason I agree.

I'm reading to Gavin when I hear a knock at the door. Will is a few minutes early. Before I can rise from the chair, David is at the door, opening it. "Hi! You must be Will. Come on in." I'm stunned. David, it seems, has forgotten that he's my kid. Apparently, he thinks he's my father.

"And you must be David," Will says, smiling and shaking my boy's hand. "How are you, mate?"

I introduce Gavin, who says hello and then is happy to be ushered upstairs to bed.

By the time I get back downstairs, David and Will are deep in conversation. I'm shocked. David hardly had the time of day for Griff.

A week later, Will comes by again to pick me up, and again, he and David start chatting. Though Will and I had intended to go out for a drink again, it takes quite a while to get out the door.

The third time Will comes by, Gavin peeks his head down the stairs. "Can I come down and visit for a while?" he asks.

It's a grey afternoon in mid-December, a Sunday without kids. I'm sitting at the kitchen table, watching Will at work. There's a chicken curry simmering on the stove and the room is filled with the spicy aromas of roasted cumin and coriander. Will is lost in his own world, quietly singing to himself as he slices onions and grinds fresh-roasted spices. I can see that he's in his element.

"How did you learn to cook?" I ask.

He looks up from his work. "I don't know," he says. "Watching Mum. She cooked beautifully. Curries, sambals, the dishes she grew up with in Sri Lanka."

"Did she teach you?"

He laughs. "When I left home, I couldn't boil an egg." He pauses and then continues. "But I knew the flavours, the aromas. I just messed about until I got it right."

"It smells amazing."

He smiles. “I’m not finished yet. I still need to finish the dahl, and make the sambal.” He tells me about the fresh coconut chutney his mum made for him whenever he went home; how cooking was the way she showed her love.

“What a lovely way to remember her, making the food she made for you.”

He nods. “And now I do the same as she did, cooking for my son. For you.”

I’m touched by his words, but before I can respond, he grins and says, “Now, can I get back to my cooking? I can’t stand around and chat all day.”

He sees me withdraw and laughs. “Oh, Darlin’,” he says, coming over to hug me, “I’m just teasing you.” He gives me a kiss before he gets back to work.

"I'm not quite sure what you see in me," Will says to me one day. "I'm just an ordinary bloke."

Yep. No sports car. No sail boat. And a sense of humour that is decidedly adolescent. An ordinary bloke.

But Will seems to have won over my children effortlessly; he's invited me into his life, introducing me early to his friends and colleagues. He never leaves me guessing about how he feels. "I can't wait to see you again," he tells me when we haven't seen one another for a couple of days. "I am seriously in like with you."

He is devoted to his son, softening whenever he speaks about his boy, and I know how much he's given up much to be able to raise him. He's a man who misses his mother, who remembers her with affection and tells little stories about the ways she showed her love. And he's fiercely loyal to his friends.

Is he perfect?

No. He is complex, flawed, and real. Just like me.

An ordinary bloke. One, I think, who might be worth hanging on to.

Things between us seem promising enough that just before Christmas, we go away for a long weekend together. We escape to the west coast of Vancouver Island, to a wild stretch of long beaches, mostly deserted at this time of year, and buffeted by wind and huge winter waves. It's my favourite place in the world, a place that I love especially during storm season. We choose a lovely hotel built right over the water from which we can watch the December storms roll in one after another. It should be idyllic.

But whether it's because things are heating up between us or because it's the first time we've spent a few days together, I start to feel jittery and uncertain. I find myself irritated with Will because he doesn't want to come out on a hike with me one afternoon, even though the weather is alternating between hail storms and freezing rain. I'm cranky that he's brought along a movie that he wants us to watch together, when I want to sit in front of the fireplace and talk. It's as though all of a sudden, he can't do anything right.

One afternoon, we're walking my very favourite beach, a place I've been coming to since I was little. I've brought along my camera, and I'm photographing the beach and the moody sky. Will is holding back, walking a little way behind me and I find myself really annoyed.

"What's wrong? Why don't you want to walk with me?" My voice is laced with irritation.

Will looks confused. "I just wanted to give you some space to take your photographs."

"We're in this beautiful, romantic place, and you won't even walk with me and hold my hand." I can hear how unreasonable I sound even as the words are coming out of my mouth.

Will observes me for a long moment and then laughs. "You are a princess sometimes, aren't you?" He comes over, wraps his arms around me and gives me a kiss. "Okay, my liege. Your wish is my command. Let me take your hand. I will walk this beach with you as you wish."

Even with his skill in defusing conflict, Will can't avoid my ire, and we find ourselves at odds a number of times during what was meant to be a romantic getaway.

It's Christmas time and the boys and I are at my mother's house for a family celebration. As our big family dinner begins, my uncle raises his glass. "To Gordon," he says. We all take a moment to remember Dad, clinking glasses across the table. I feel a lump in my throat and feel tears threatening, and I can see across the table my sister is struggling too. I feel Dad's absence the most at times like this, when we're all together.

Throughout the evening, though, we feel his presence. As my sister and her husband tease Gavin, I know Dad would be in the middle of it. As my uncle and my mom talk rugby and cricket, I can guess at Dad's opinions.

And throughout dinner, I'm also aware of how effortlessly Will would fit in with my family.

After dinner, my sister and I are cleaning up together. "So when are we going to meet this new man?" she asks.

"Oh, I don't know. It felt a bit soon to be inviting him to a family dinner."

"He sounds like a good guy, though."

"You'd really like him. He's so like Dad."

"Really?" she laughs.

"In good ways and bad. He's got Dad's warmth and humour. But also, he can't ever keep track of his keys or his glasses." My sister starts to laugh.

"I'd love to meet him."

"Yeah. Maybe one of these days." I hesitate. "I'm just not sure about him yet."

She looks at me and shakes her head. "When can you ever be absolutely sure about someone? At some point you have to take a chance."

I shrug. "I don't know..."

She looks at me hard. "When are you going to let somebody love you again?"

Her question slaps me. I feel my throat tighten, the tears welling up. She sees I'm upset and reaches to hug me.

"I'm so done with heartbreak."

She's crying now too. "But how long are you going to be alone? You don't want that for your life."

I'm sitting in Linda's office after Christmas, feeling miserable. "I don't understand why I do this. As soon as I start getting close to somebody, I start creating distance. I can feel myself focusing on Will's flaws, magnifying them; it's like I'm cataloguing them, building a case for why he isn't the right man for me."

Linda nods. "Where are your reservations?"

I shrug. "He is not at all outdoorsy. This is not a man I'm ever going kayaking with."

Linda waits for me to go on.

"He watches way too much TV. I don't even know how to turn my TV on. And he hasn't got a romantic bone in his body."

"And these are all things you need to weigh. But are they deal- breakers?"

"I don't know," I sigh. "Also he's got a completely adolescent sense of humour. It seems impossible for him to have a serious conversation without cracking jokes. Sometimes it feels like it's his way of keeping distance from me."

Linda smiles gently. "Sounds like you're both putting up a few guards."

"Yeah. He might be even better at protecting his heart than I am. I'm the first woman he's gotten involved with since his divorce – and that was more than seven years ago."

"So you're both guarded. No surprise there."

"I just wish I could be kinder. Even as I say something critical or contrary, I know I'm doing it, but it's like I can't stop myself."

"Self protection is a powerful instinct." She lets that idea sink in. "What might be at play for you?"

"I'm sure I'm trying to hold distance between us."

"Because?"

I pause, thinking this through. "Will's the first guy I could see integrating fully into my life. He gets along great with my kids. I know he'd get along with my mom and my sister. He's already friends with my friend Kim and I know he'd get along with my other friends too."

"It's what you most want and most fear."

I laugh. "Exactly! I can't just keep Will all to myself. If I want what he's offering, I'll have to invite him into my whole life."

"It's the ultimate in vulnerability for you, allowing someone access to your whole life and your most precious people."

I nod, feeling miserable. "It scares the hell out of me. But there's so much that I really like about him. He totally gets me. He appreciates about me the things I value the most about myself.

Linda smiles and lets me continue.

"I actually went back in my journal to the spring and found a list of qualities I wanted in my next partner. It's like I was describing Will. Someone who's kind, warm, easy-going. Fun. Intelligent. Someone who accepts me as I am, who wants to share his life with me. Someone who likes my kids. Someone loyal and steady."

Linda smiles again. "Sounds like there's lots of good here." She waits for a moment before continuing. "So try not to be ruled by fear. Try not to make judgments. Just focus on gathering information. Just notice who he is and how he treats you. It will become clear, but it's too soon to know yet."

# TWENTY-TWO

# GIVING THINGS A CHANCE

Through the last days of December and into early January, I try to remember Linda's advice. Rather than getting caught up in the anxiety of indecision, I try to just gather information and pay attention to how Will treats me.

He is not a man of grand gestures and heartfelt pronouncements. But he'll spend an entire afternoon preparing an aromatic curry dinner for me. He'll head out into the winter rain with Gavin to coach him on how to kick a rugby ball. He'll listen patiently to Luke's explanation about the latest thing he's learned on the Internet. "Did you know, Will," Luke will begin, before launching into an account of how Pluto was demoted to the status of dwarf planet. I'll watch the exchange, waiting for Will to catch my eye, raise his eyebrows and smile, and then turn his patient attention back to my youngest son.

The boys love when he's around. He shares stories about growing up with his three wild brothers in Australia, reinforcing how well behaved my boys are. He tells jokes that only a fourteen year-old boy could appreciate. And he encourages farting. When Gavin lets one go at the dinner table, I turn and give him the death glare, but Will just winks at him, and says, "Nice one."

My boys are entranced.

Early in January, Will arrives one evening distraught. I can tell something is wrong as soon as I open the door. He gathers me in a big hug and tells me his news still holding on to me. "My mate Gary died," he says, his voice choking.

"Gary? Who lives in Vancouver?"

He nods. "Heart attack. Two nights ago. It took them a couple of days to track me down."

"Two nights ago? He called you that night." I remembered Will smiling as he listened to his old friend's message.

"He died a couple of hours after he called."

I hold on to Will, knowing there's nothing I can say. He and Gary had been friends since they were teenagers in the same small town in Australia, and for the last ten years or so, they'd both been in Canada, living only hours away from each other. Their life-long friendship had only intensified on Canadian soil.

Will spends the evening sharing stories about Gary with me. Over the years, the two of them had gotten themselves into all kinds of trouble, but underneath the silliness, was history, loyalty, and love. Gary's death would be a huge loss for Will. "I wish you could have met him," Will says. "You would have adored him." Based on some of the stories Will has told me, I'm not entirely sure. Gary had been a lifelong bachelor, frequently juggling more than one woman at a time. "But that's why you'd have loved him," Will tells me, laughing at his friend. "He was so utterly charming."

I accompany Will to Gary's funeral the following week and I'm struck by the layers of tragedy. It's so sad that Gary has died so young, and that Will has lost a dear mate, the one friend in Canada who'd known him since he was young. But there is tragedy, too, in Gary dying so far from home. His sisters fly in, but his parents are too frail to make the long journey. It's clear from the many Canadian friends at the funeral that Gary has made a life for himself here. But he'd never settled down. He didn't have a partner or children there to mourn his passing. Instead, as Will has warned, there are a number of women, current and former girlfriends, who arrive to pay their respects.

Will delivers a eulogy that is at once heartfelt and funny, sharing carefully curated stories from their days together in Australia. As I sit and listen, I am so glad for Gary's family that there is a dear friend from home remembering their brother and their son. I'm proud of Will for the speech he delivers, for his ability to share so eloquently a part of Gary's story that many at the service wouldn't know. I'm proud that he is so self-possessed, knowing how much he misses his mate.

Will's loss shifts the focus for us, and for a while, my anxiety lessens. I'm too concerned about how Will is doing to be worrying about whether he's the right guy for me. Through January, I see how devoted Will is to the people he loves, how sad he is about Gary's death, how big his heart is. I think back to the palm reader. Here, I know, is a man who could protect my heart.

As Valentine's Day approaches, I find myself more and more jittery. I catalogue Will's virtues in my journal, a reminder for myself of all that is good. But I find myself focussing on the things that are worrying me, the things that seem too hard this early in a relationship.

"What's going on?" Will asks one Sunday afternoon as we're out walking his dog.

I pause, not sure whether to begin. I'm worried about where a conversation like this will end. But I start anyway. "This just feels too heavy. We've only been going out a few months. I feel like this early on, it should be easy." I stop myself from saying more.

Will pauses before speaking. "Darlin', we're not twenty anymore. Our lives are complicated. We've got kids and jobs. We're both pretty set in our ways. You can't expect it to be easy."

"But three months in, I want to feel swept away, like none of the obstacles matter."

Will laughs and hugs me. "We are meant to be together. I absolutely know that. I adore you and I'm okay with the hard parts."

I'm silent for a while. "I don't know if I'm okay, though. I'm struggling. I don't want things to feel so hard."

Will sighs. "Tell me the things that are bugging you."

I'm not sure where to begin. "I hate that we have so little time together. I wish we could go out together on the weekends more, socialize more with friends."

"You know I have Simon from Wednesday to Saturday. He's my son. That's precious time for me." I sense Will's defensiveness right away.

"I know. And it's not like I'm available all the time either. My schedule with the boys is pretty busy too. It's just hard, that's all."

But he surprises me. "If it's important to you, I'll see if Simon's mom can have him sometimes on a Friday or a Saturday."

"Thank you." I smile at him, but I'm still feeling sad. There are so many other little things that are still worrying me.

"What else?" Will says, picking up on my mood. He waits for me to keep going.

And we launch into a difficult conversation about our differences and about the difficulties of beginning a relationship at midlife.

Later, as we're having dinner in the local Vietnamese restaurant, Will asks, "How are you feeling now?"

I smile. "Better. Thank you."

He reaches across the table for my hand. "You're alright, you are," he says, putting on his broadest Aussie accent. "I think you're going to like the movie I've picked for tonight."

We watch *The Adventures of Priscilla, Queen of the Desert,* a movie I vaguely remember from when it first came out. But watching it with a man who calls Australia home gives it new meaning, and I'm particularly taken with a scene at the end of the movie. One of the characters, Bernadette, elects to stay in Alice Springs with the mechanic she's fallen in love with.

Her friends ask her if she's sure about this decision.

"No," she replies, "I'm not sure. But how can I find out if I don't give it a chance?"

At this, Will pulls me closer to him and squeezes my shoulder, and I smile at him. "Good advice," he says, kissing my forehead.

As we're falling asleep that night, Will whispers, "Let's just let this last as long as it's meant to, Darlin'"

There is wisdom in his words.

"I am a complete mess," I tell Linda the next time I'm in her office. "All I want is to know for certain what to do."

She smiles sympathetically and lets me continue.

"Here is a guy who is loyal and faithful. He gets along with my kids, with my friends. He's ready to make a full commitment. It's exactly what I wanted."

"And...."

"And I'm so confused. How do I know if Will is the right guy for me? How can I be sure that I'm not making another in a long string of relationship mistakes?" I take a deep breath, knowing that I'm starting to sound a little hysterical. "I so badly don't want to make another mistake. I want to know that I won't end up getting my heart broken again. That I won't break someone else's heart."

"Does Will know that you're struggling?"

"Yes. He's been steady and solid and loving. He's stepped back and given me space. It just makes me feel worse that he's being so understanding."

Linda nods and waits for me to go on.

"I just want to feel absolutely certain. Hell Yes! You know?"

She smiles. "Complete certainty is a pretty big ask."

"I guess. It just doesn't feel exciting enough. It all seems so calm and stable –"

"So ordinary?" She's smiling again.

"Yes! I feel like I should be swept away at this point, like I'm settling if I don't feel swept away."

"Calm and stable *is* healthy," Linda reminds me. "It might take you some time to re-learn that after your last relationship. You got the really big highs with Griff, all that excitement and romance, but it came with really big lows too."

I think about this. "Yeah. I never knew when he was going to bolt. But how do I know if I'm making the right decision? Am I settling if I end up with a guy who won't come backpacking with me? Am I settling if I don't feel swept away?"

Linda waits until I finish. "You may want to think about settling a little differently, Sally. When you settle into an armchair, you're choosing to be comfortable. Settling can be about comfort and security and steadiness."

I let that sink in.

Linda continues. "Give this relationship time. You need time to learn again what healthy feels like."

"But I'm so stressed out!"

She nods.

"I guess that's probably fear speaking. Right?"

She nods again. "It's perfectly natural that you'd be feeling fearful right now."

"But what if it isn't fear? What if I'm not paying attention to my body's deep wisdom?"

"You're anxious. That's normal. But it doesn't mean you have to do anything about it."

"But I just want to make that anxiety go away."

She smiles at me. "Try to just relax. Stay open. You don't have to make a decision right now. You don't have enough information yet to make a decision."

Even though I trust Linda's advice, I can't follow it, and within weeks I call things off.

*Dear Will,*

*I wish I knew how to end a relationship gracefully. I wish it could be done without hurt and without anger. I know I've hurt you and I am so sorry.*

*I wish I could explain in a way that would make sense to you why I needed to end things. There was so much that was good about our developing relationship. And there is so much that is good about you. But I have to listen to my heart, Will.*

*I believe that there are gifts in every relationship, no matter how brief. You have shown me what it feels like to be loved in a way that is solid and grounded. It's been years since I've felt that way, years since I've really been able to trust somebody fully. From the beginning, I knew my heart was safe with you.*

*And you've shown me that I don't need to keep a romantic relationship entirely separate from my family life. One of the things I loved about you the most was the way you interacted with my kids. I haven't told them yet about this ending. I know they're going to miss you.*

*And I'm going to miss you too, Will. There's so much I'm going to miss about you.*

*I'm so sorry. You risked your heart for me. I wish that I could have protected your heart the way I know you would have protected mine. I hope that you will risk it again, Will. You are a good man. You deserve the happiness of a strong relationship.*
*I wish I could have given you a kiss goodbye.*
*Sally*

In the days following the break up, I alternate between feeling guilty for the abrupt way I ended things with Will and feeling deeply relieved that I've finally done so. Throughout January and February, I had spent hours every day obsessing about whether Will was the right man for me. I couldn't just relax and let things unfold. I was incapable of just seeing where things might take us. I couldn't handle the uncertainty and wanted to know *absolutely for sure* that I was doing the right thing. It's my pattern. When things are particularly uncertain in my life, I clamp down and do everything I can to stay in control. This was a situation that was by its very nature uncertain. How can any of us know for certain that we're getting involved with somebody who will be good for us? But instead of accepting my anxiety, I bolted. This, of course, is very easy for me to see in retrospect. In the moment, I finally felt like I could breathe again. I didn't doubt my decision for a minute.

"I can't believe how relieved I feel," I tell Kira when we're having coffee a few days later. "I feel so much better."

"Don't you miss him?"

"I do. But I couldn't handle how horrible I was feeling. I was sick with anxiety."

"You know," Kira starts. "I've been reading all those self-help books? I think I'm on number fourteen or something."

"You must be the most well-adjusted woman in Canada by now!"

"Yeah, except every time I finish one, it leads me to something else I need to figure out about myself."

"Don't you think that after all we've been through we should be done? Complete? Perfectly happy and balanced and all that?"

"I know. We should be." She pauses. "I think you should read one of the books on my list. It's about commitment."

"Me?"

"Maybe. It might give you some insight."

But I'm not really interested in insight. I am just so relieved that I've ended things with Will and that I'm not feeling that constant sense of anxiety. I feel so calm now, and that sense of calm is all I need to know I've done the right thing.

I am sad, it's true. I know I've said goodbye to a good man, and I know I've hurt him in the process. I'm also sad for my boys, because they really liked Will, and though they don't say very much, I can tell they're upset. More than anything, I'm angry with myself. *I should never have introduced him to the boys,* I think. I saw how hard it was for them to weather their parents' separation, and I didn't want them to have to go through that ever again. More than anything, I wanted to protect them from any more pain. But I let them get to know and to like Will, and now I can see that they're hurting too.

Over the next month, I keep myself busy at work and at home with the boys, who are with me for a longer stretch while their dad is away on business. When Spring Break comes around, I take them away for a few days to the beach. It's good to get away, to have some time with just the four of us. We play games together, head to the pool, and take long, windy walks along the beach. I have a picture of us on the beach together from that little holiday, my little family of four, a reminder of how carefully I have crafted a new definition of family after my divorce, how comfortable the four of us are as a unit. Looking at our smiling faces, I wonder why I had even tried to find somebody who could fit in with my family. We are perfectly happy the way we are.

I also spend time with Kira and Matt, both of whom know what it's like to be single in one's forties and out in the dating pool. I love them both for their perspective, but also because they make me laugh.

"I can't explain how relieved I feel," I tell Matt as we're out for a walk together shortly after the breakup. "I feel so good! It just makes me wonder why I didn't end things sooner."

"Yeah, I know what you mean." Matt has recently broken up with somebody too, so I'm expecting a reflection on his latest experience. "Sometimes," he says, "I get that same feeling after I've been playing solitaire on the computer for too long. I get off the computer and I can't believe that I've spent so much time doing something so mindless."

I laugh at his meanderings. "It's not like I feel like I wasted my time. I learned a huge amount going out with Will. It's just that I felt so crappy at the end."

"Kind of like too much solitaire." He grins at me and continues. "You are really not able to handle discomfort, are you?"

I sigh. "No."

"I think you're going to have to get through that uncomfortable stage with somebody at some point."

"Yeah. Probably."

"Or you could do like me," Matt adds, "and just give up on dating altogether. I'm done with it for a while."

I'm not so sure that I am, though.

# TWENTY-THREE

# X IS FOR XAVIER AND Y IS FOR YAN

Perhaps unwisely, I find my way back to *Plenty of Fish*. I know I should probably spend a little more time getting centered, but I'm beginning to understand that in the same way that other people escape with television or shopping, I avoid facing my hurt and loneliness with online dating. The attention is nice, but so is the busy-ness. When it's not making me crazy, *Plenty of Fish* is a supremely effective distraction from real life.

Shortly after I open my profile, Xavier contacts me. I think he's new to the site, because I haven't seen him before and I'm immediately interested. He's a life coach and his profile is positive and reflective. Immediately I think, *This is someone on the same page as me.*

Xavier and I meet at a funky little coffee shop and both order lattes. As we talk, he leans back in his chair, obviously at ease, and looking comfortable in a dress shirt and jeans. Could I go out, I wonder, with a man with piercings? I'm pretty sure I've never dated a man with earrings before. I wonder briefly whether he has tattoos. But it wouldn't be polite to ask. *Stop judging*, I tell myself. Xavier tells me about his midlife career change. "It's been a bit touch and go for me," he admits, "but coaching just feels like exactly what I'm meant to be doing."

Xavier is personable and warm, and I can see his enthusiasm for life as he tells me a little about himself. As I suspected, we are on the same page. We share a political perspective that is decidedly left of center. We are both dedicated to self-growth. We both value family. Xavier is so passionate about single parenting that he runs a support group for single dads. I can't help admiring him.

I'm a little concerned about the lack of financial stability in his life, but he is so likeable, so passionate about his work, that I have no doubt he'll eventually be successful.

As I finish my latte, I realize that here is another man who would probably be really good for me. Despite the piercings, he's an attractive man with a lovely, warm smile.

And I don't feel even the slightest attraction.

*Stay open*, I tell myself, and agree to meet for a drink later in the week.

*Hi Xavier,*
*It was lovely to get to know you. You are a guy who is making a difference in the world and somebody who is living a big life. I admire those things about you. But it doesn't feel as though we are headed towards a romantic relationship. I really hope that you find the right woman soon*
*Sally*

After Xavier, I come across Yan's profile. In his photo, he looks like he's just wandered out of a J. Crew catalogue, a tall, fit looking man, all sun bleached hair and faded khakis. Not only is he good looking, but also he has a Ph.D. I'm tempted to contact him, except for the toddler. Although my youngest son is only eight, I can't quite imagine dealing once more with a two year old. The other thing is that this man is younger than me, better educated, and unquestionably, he's prettier too. I'm not sure if a man this beautiful will deign to respond to me, but I think, "What the hell!" and send him a message.

"Now I'm not sure whether you have a complete understanding of game theory," Yan says to me as he strides along the waterfront, me walking quickly to try to keep up. It's a beautiful day in late April when I meet Yan. The sun is warm and scatters sparkles across the very blue ocean. Yan is every bit as good looking as his pictures suggest; I'm glad that I've taken extra care with my appearance. He's also every bit as smart as his Ph.D. would suggest and I'm wracking my brains for anything I can remember about game theory. I come up blank.

"Um, no. You'll have to give me a quick overview," I say.

He launches into an enthusiastic explanation, and then shares with me the connections between game theory and divorce. "It's quite fascinating, don't you think?" he asks.

"It is," I agree, even though I'm still back trying to sort out the basics of game theory, and have missed most of his explanation about how it relates to divorce. He's charming, this man, smiley and animated, and obviously passionate about many things. He's already told me about his doctoral research and the projects he's currently working on, about his years at university, and about how he met and eventually split with his first wife. He's an entertaining storyteller and I find myself laughing and prompting him to share other parts of his life. He tells me about his years growing up in California, and from there, he tells me all about his brothers. He tells me about his daughter and his struggles to balance his emerging career with the responsibilities of parenting. He talks about his travels.

The afternoon sunshine is warm and we walk a long way. We've been walking for about two hours, when I realize he hasn't stopped talking, and hasn't asked me anything about myself. It isn't that he comes across as self-absorbed or arrogant, which is perhaps why it takes so long for me to notice the pattern. He just seems happy to talk and oblivious that it's a two way process.

I make a conscious effort to not ask him another question, and wait to see what will happen. As he finishes a story about his time in Africa, there's a moment of silence, and I deliberately remain quiet. He pauses a moment and then says, "I don't know if you've been to Asia..." Before I have a chance to respond, he adds, "but in many ways I found it more fascinating than my time in Africa." And he's off again.

*Hi Yan,*
*Thanks for spending your afternoon with me. It was a beautiful day for walking Dallas Road and for sitting on the beach in the sunshine. It feels like I learned a tremendous amount about you in our afternoon together. Perhaps if we do this again, I'll tell you a little more about me.*
*All the best,*
*Sally*

"So I'm avoiding going out on another date," I tell Kira. We're sitting in our favourite coffee shop, the brick walls glowing in the afternoon sun. I take a sip of my latte, and sigh. "I've dated my way right to the end of the alphabet. All I have left is *Z is for Zak*!"

Kira laughs. "That's actually pretty impressive. Twenty-five dates in a year. Not bad for someone who has a full time job and three kids!"

I laugh too. "And if you add up all the dating over the last few years, I'm up past fifty. I should win an award!"

"You should write a book. *Dating Wisdom from the Trenches.*"

"Yeah. Except I'm still single. Obviously I don't have a whole lot of wisdom to share." I pause. "According to the wise folks at *Plenty of Fish*, it takes an average of seven dates to find someone."

"Clearly, they haven't factored your dating patterns into their calculations."

"Or yours," I laugh. "But here's what I'm worrying about. What am I going to do about my blog? I need a new plan. I'm at the end of the alphabet. What am I going to do after Zak? Or Zeb?"

Kira looks at me thoughtfully. "How about theme months? June could be men under fifty who love motorcycles and dancing. In July you could date only men who pose in front of their cars."

"Or boats." I'm laughing again.

"Or you could date by astrological sign. June could be the month of Capricorn."

"Apparently I should be dating Cancers and Scorpios. Don't even ask me how I know this."

"Or!" Kira looks triumphant. "Or you could start a new cycle. *A is for Andrea!*"

With all the laughter, we're attracting the attention of the other people in the coffee shop now. "That might work. One of my lesbian friends already sent me an email signed *J is for Jen.*"

As Kira comes up with more ridiculous suggestions, I realize that maybe in playing *The Alphabet Dating Game,* I've created a self-fulfilling prophecy. The minute I wrote *A is for Adam,* I ensured that I'd still be writing about dating at the end of the alphabet. It's been my experience that the universe provides exactly what I ask for. It's just that usually I don't realize until it's too late that I've put in a request.

Now that I think about it, maybe I can use that self-fulfilling concept to my benefit. Maybe I can get the universe working on my behalf.

I stop Kira. "Do you think it's too late for me to become a trophy wife?"

# TWENTY-FOUR

# Z IS FOR ZAK

Zak's message arrives in my inbox on a day when I'm feeling particularly low. I'm convinced that there are no men left in the city worth dating, that I've dated every last one. And there is some crazy part of me that thinks that when I go out on the "Z" date, that will be it. My dating days will be over. Irrational, I know. But it has stopped me from responding to a number of men who I might otherwise have taken the chance of a coffee date.

Zak's message is funny and self-effacing, enough to spark my curiosity. I check out his profile, and see a handsome man smiling out at me.

A handsome man in uniform. Zak is in the military.

I don't date men in uniform. It's sort of like my irrational little rule about men who are teachers. I don't have any good reason for this uniform rule, except that I am afraid of guns and don't like the idea of going out with somebody who has to strap on a gun before he heads out to work. Police officers? Out. Men in the military? No way. I'm ready to close the profile, but a voice inside whispers, *Stay open*. I sigh in exasperation, and read Zak's profile.

He's an engineer. Probably he doesn't have to use a gun very often at all if he's an engineer. Even if he's in the military.

I read further and see that he's been transferred to the West Coast and has been here for a year. That's when I remember the other reason I don't date military: they get transferred. And I have no intention of moving.

"You don't have to marry the guy," that annoying little voice reminds me. "Stay open."

And as I read over Zak's profile, I have to admit that he seems like an interesting guy. I can tell from the way he writes that he's funny and intelligent, and it sounds like he's lead an interesting life, travelling around the world for his work, and living abroad for long stretches.

I send a quick reply.

"Now tell me a little bit about you," Zak says, striding confidently along the muddy trail circling Thetis Lake. This is his regular circuit and he's moving fast, but so far I've been able to keep up. I've been doing my usual thing, which is to keep the conversation going by asking one question after another, and Zak has played the game for a while, cheerfully sharing stories about his kids and his career and his adventures overseas. He's a lively storyteller, with good material, and I suspect that he quite likes sharing his tales. But he's on to me. And now I have to talk. Zak is as good a listener as he is a storyteller and he in no time, it seems, we've completed the ten kilometre circuit and have arrived back at the parking lot.

"That was fun," Zak says as I reach my car.

"It was." I smile.

"Say," he starts, a grin on his face. "What do you think about meeting me for an ice cream at Beacon Hill Park some time, and then we could feed the ducks? I love ducks!"

I laugh at his boyish zeal, looking forward already to meeting up with Zak again.

Together, Zak and I feed the ducks. We meet again and walk along Dallas Road. We get together twice for dinner at his place. And every time we meet, we have interesting conversations and lots of laughs. I like his energy, his many enthusiasms, and his easy way with me. I can even forgive his right wing political views.

But while there is good energy between us, I feel myself holding back. I like Zak, but here's another guy that I'm not really sure I want to kiss. And either he feels the same way, or is politely waiting for an invitation. It's an invitation I'm not offering. And I don't know why.

After our fifth date, after dinner and a glass of wine and a long evening of conversation, I push myself up from the couch. All evening I've sat at one end and he at the other. "I should get going," I say.

"Okay then," he says, smiling and getting up too.

"Thanks for the lovely evening. And the Shake and Bake." I'm laughing.

"I can't believe that I'm the first man to ever serve you Shake and Bake on a date!" He's laughing too.

He helps me into my coat and there is an awkward moment at the door. "Well, good night. Thanks again." And I'm out the door. Five dates and we haven't even kissed. It's kind of weird.

*Dear Zak,*
*I have really enjoyed spending time with you and getting to know you. I'm going to miss your light heart and your great sense of humour. I hope that just around the next corner is a girl who is perfect for you. May she love golf. May she love rock and roll. May she love feeding the ducks.*
*Warmest wishes,*
*Sally*

I'm feeling demoralized as I write to Zak. Intellectually, I know that Z doesn't mark the end of my dating adventures, but I can't quite believe that I've been on twenty-six dates in just over a year – and that I still haven't found the right guy. I'm tired of the whole online dating process and I'm wondering what's wrong with me.

"My parents met in a teeny little town," I say to Kira when I see her next. "It's not like they had a whole lot of choice. And they were happy!"

"Yeah. I think all that choice is part of the problem," Kira says. "It's so easy to discard one guy for the possibility of the next. And there's a seemingly endless supply of men out there."

"Not really, though. Narrow down to the ones who are somewhere in the same age range –"

"And have a few shared interests –"

"And don't have any obvious addiction issues –"

We're laughing again.

"And then what are the chances that they're in the right space to meet someone?" I add, thinking of Tom, who went out with me when he should have still been going out with his evil twin.

"Or that we're ready either," Kira adds, raising her eyebrows at me.

"Yeah, I know. I was not exactly prime dating material when I started dating again."

"Have you read that book yet?" Kira asks.

I sigh. "Give me the name again."

# TWENTY-FIVE

# HELL YES

"So apparently I have problems with commitment," I tell Linda, showing her Kira's book.

Linda smiles. "We all have problems with commitment to one degree or another."

"No. This guy describes me perfectly." I flip to a dog-eared page and read about people who choose unavailable partners. "That's Andrew, the first man I dated after my divorce. He lived a two-hour drive and a two-hour ferry ride away. A nice, safe distance. And it also describes Griff. I knew when I met him that he was never going to fit into my whole life."

"Those choices reflect where you were in your emotional journey, Sally. It doesn't mean that you have always and will always be afraid to commit."

I flip to another page. I read out a section about how people with commitment issues can't handle open, available people.

"Look at Ben. Look at Will. Totally good guys, ready to commit. And I couldn't get away from them fast enough."

Linda's nodding thoughtfully. "A place on your journey."

"And do you remember how crazy I felt with Will? How I was so anxious and wound up? And how relieved I felt once I broke up with him?" I hold up the book again. "This guy describes exactly the same thing!"

Linda is smiling again in that disconcerting, therapist way. "And does this author suggest how to overcome your fear of commitment?"

"Uh, yeah," I mumble, unable to make eye contact. "Basically to do what you told me to do." I'm a bit embarrassed having to admit this. "Relax. Take things slow. Don't bolt just because you're feeling uncomfortable."

"And that sense of anxiety will eventually pass," Linda adds.

Early in May, Will sends me a text. *Any chance of a coffee? I have a couple of things to drop off to you and I wouldn't mind catching up.*

I've been feeling guilty about the way things ended with Will, the way I sent him off so abruptly. I hate those kinds of endings. I'd like to apologize. So I invite him over.

*Sunday afternoon? Come and have a beer in the back garden.*

He shows up looking tanned and healthy, dressed in shorts and a golf shirt.

"I was out having a hit of golf," he says, gesturing to the outfit. As I pull a couple of beers out of the fridge, he tells me about the game, a bit of small talk to mask our discomfort.

"How are the boys," he asks, once we're sitting out back. I can see the fondness for them in his expression.

"Good," I start, and fill him in on the boys' lives in the months since we've spoken.

"And Simon?" I ask, about his son. Will fills me in.

There's an awkward silence when he finishes talking.

"Look," I say, "I'm really sorry about the way I ended things with you. I wish I could have done it in a way that was kinder. Not so abrupt."

He sighs. "Thanks. It was a bit of a surprise." The master of understatement.

"I didn't really plan to break up with you that day," I said. "I'd been trying to just stay in the moment and not panic. But I just couldn't do it any longer." I look at him to make sure he's listening. "I'm really sorry, Will. I didn't want to hurt you."

There's a long silence between us, before Will speaks. "Look," he says, "I didn't come here today to try and change your mind."

"No. It was the right thing that we ended things."

"I don't agree," he says, smiling at me gently. "But I respect your decision." He pauses. "I wanted you to know that I've had to take a hard look at myself over the last couple of months and really make some changes."

"You're golfing again," I said. "That's good."

"Golfing. Working out. Reading again. Even doing a bit of writing."

I let him go on. "I was in a pretty negative place. I see that now. You were right that I needed to do some things for myself."

"You look good, Will. Tanned, relaxed. You look happy."

He nods, and starts telling me about the book he's just finished reading, by one of the Indian authors we both admire.

As I listen to him, I feel my guard dropping. Before me, I see the man that I fell in love with back in November, and I'm surprised by the realization.

In the months since we split up, I have been convinced that I did the right thing in ending things with Will. I've felt guilty about the messy ending, but I haven't felt regret about the actual decision.

He must sense the change because he stops talking and just looks at me for a long minute. "I've missed you," he says softly, and reaches over to take my hand.

Though things with Will might not be as completely over as I'd imagined, I'm not ready to jump back into a relationship with him. If I've learned anything, it's that I need to slow things down. We agree to meet the following week, without placing any expectation on the meeting.

"I can't just jump back in," I tell Will. "And I'm not sharing any of this with my boys. They were so sad that we broke up in the first place."

"Let's just see how things unfold," Will says.

I'm surprised to feel first-date nervous when we meet for our hike, and I think he's nervous too. We're probably five kilometres around the lake before I begin to feel comfortable, but after that, Will and I laugh and talk as though we'd never broken up. Near the end, Will takes my hand. "Let's do this again, okay?"

Over the next month, we meet for walks and for movies, and it feels good that we've found our way back to an amicable, if not quite clear, place together. I'm particularly grateful for the change, as the middle-school rugby season has begun. As Gavin plays, and Will coaches for another local school, we see each other regularly at games and tournaments. I can't even imagine how uncomfortable it would be if we weren't speaking to each other. As it is, we can smile and say hello, and engage in a little bit of middle-school rugby rivalry. At tournaments, Will sometimes comes over and watches Gavin play. "He's a solid little player," he says. "He could be very good." It's at times like this that I wonder what it would be like to have Will as my partner.

In June, Will and I are still in an in-between place. I've said nothing to the boys and very little to my friends. Without the pressure of being in a relationship, I can just enjoy Will's company. I'm not worrying about whether he's the right guy for me and nor am I cataloguing his virtues and his faults. It's a lovely place to be, but I know that sooner or later, we're going to have to make a decision about our next steps.

One afternoon, I'm waiting for Gavin to get his gear together so that I can take him to rugby tryouts for a regional rep team. "Come on, buddy," I shout up the stairs. "You don't want to be late."

He comes out of his room looking distressed. "I can't find my mouth guard anywhere."

"When did you have it last? Is it at Dad's?"

"No. I had it at the city finals. I came back here with you that day."

Together we search the house, but I can see his panic rising and time is ticking away.

I call Will. He laughs when I explain the situation, knowing Gavin's propensity for losing things. "You'll be able to get one in the local drugstore," he says, "but call me back if there's a problem."

"Gav, let's go," I say. "I know where we can get a mouth guard." I see the relief wash over Gavin's face.

But the local drugstore does not have any mouth guards in stock and now we are really short for time.

We get into the car, and I pass Gavin my phone. "Call Will," I tell him. "Ask him if he can think of anywhere else we could get one."

"Hey Will," I hear Gavin say. "Mum said to phone you. They didn't have mouth guards at the drugstore."

I hear Will's muffled voice and then Gavin's again. "Thank you so much,' he says, relief in every word.

"What did he say?" I ask.

"He'll meet us in the parking lot. He's going to get me a mouth guard."

The tryouts are at Will's school, but even still, I have no idea how he's going to find a mouth guard in the next half an hour. When we pull into the parking lot, just before 4:00, I see Will waiting for us. He has a mouth guard in one hand and a mug in the other. As Gavin steps out of the car, Will grins and hands him the mouth guard. "You're something else, mate," he says laughing. "How many of these have you lost this year?"

Gavin smiles ruefully. "Thank you."

"No worries. Let's get it into this hot water, so we can get you out onto the field." As they sort out the mouth guard, Will reassures Gavin. "I talked to your coach and he knows you're going to be a few minutes late. No need to worry, okay?" Will pats Gavin on the back before he runs out onto the field. "Good luck, mate," Will calls, and Gavin turns, pulls out the mouth guard, and gives him a big smile.

In that moment I know that this is exactly what I want in my life.

# EPILOGUE

I smile at the waiter as he places a daiquiri before me. "Gracias," I say, nearly exhausting my vast knowledge of Spanish. He smiles and nods, and places a Bucanero before Will. We've found our way to the rooftop bar of Ambos Mundos, one of Hemingway's haunts in Old Havana. The shade, the ocean breeze, and the icy drinks are a welcome relief in the heat of an August afternoon.

We've spent the day lost in the puzzle of narrow streets, wandering into old churches, resting in the shaded recesses of vast plazas, and following dusty children dancing barefoot down side streets. We've sauntered through back streets, where tired men sit in doorways, watching expressionless as we walk by. We've marvelled at the faded stateliness of the crumbling colonial buildings, at the history we stumble on throughout the city.

Will and I travel well together. We're happy to explore the city without an agenda or even a map. Neither of us is too fussy about our accommodations or the food or whether there's any hot water. We've found in one another an open and easygoing travel companion.

There is between us a sense of ease, of calm; we have the quiet confidence of trust. This, I think, is what it means to settle; it's really a *settling in*, as though we've curled up together in a big, comfortable chair.

We're happy together, but we're also learning to give one another space. Will never questions my need for solitude, for long stretches of time to write. And when I take off with the boys for a backpacking adventure, he's delighted to stay home and binge watch *House of Cards*.

We gaze out over the rooftops of Old Havana, a contented silence between us. It's unusual for us to have this time alone. Our life together now is a blur of boys and work and after-school schedules. It's a life that is beautifully ordinary. These days, Will cooks for all of us, an arrangement my boys are happy to embrace. David is away at university, but the other three boys are with us regularly on rotating and often overlapping schedules. Though it hasn't been easy, we've crafted a new definition of family, one big enough to include all our boys and a dog. With so many boys, it's also a life that includes more fart jokes than I could have anticipated. A few years ago, I couldn't have imagined a family of this shape and texture. But we've made it happen. And for the most part, it's working.

I turn to Will and smile. "I love it here. I love being here with you."

He smiles too and leans forward to kiss me.

"Wouldn't it be great to come here with the boys?" I ask.

Will laughs. "We're taking the boys to Australia next year! Cuba is just for you and me."

I look at him laughing, and think how lucky I am to have found this good man. Lifting my daiquiri to him, I smile. "Here's to whatever comes next."

# ACKNOWLEDGEMENTS

My deepest thanks first and always to Jerome. You believed in this book before I did, and encouraged me to keep writing, even if I was writing about my checkered past. Thank you, my love. I am a fortunate woman.

Loving thanks also to my boys. You are my true north. And heaven knows how I'd ever have finished this book if I hadn't had all those hours waiting at soccer, karate and rugby practices. It's remarkable how much writing I've done in parking lots.

Deep gratitude to my friends, who have supported me in so many ways. To Karen and Sylvia, thank you for your love and encouragement. You mean the world to me. To Carol and Rob, thank you for being on the dating journey with me. I don't know how I'd have survived without your humour and perspective. To the Book Sluts, thank you for witnessing my journey and cheering me on. To Karen, Carol, and Bonnie, thank you for reading early drafts of the book and for encouraging me to keep writing. And to the many friends who looked out for me, laughed with me about my dating misadventures, and encouraged me to write, thank you. I am so blessed.

Much gratitude to Tina. Thank you for your wisdom and diplomacy. It's a wonder that you've never leaped from your therapist's chair to shake me and shout, "*Are you completely out of your mind??*"

Thank you to Lionel. You are a very good dad to our boys.

Heartfelt thanks to my editor, Cate Hogan, who encouraged and pushed me in equal measures, and to Andy Ugro, who designed the beautiful book cover.

And, finally, a special thank you to the men that I dated – and sometimes wrote about. I really enjoyed meeting so many of you, and learned so much in the process. Internet dating is not for the faint of heart, so thank you for being courageous enough to put yourselves out there. I hope you've each found your own version of happily ever after.

# A NOTE ABOUT THE AUTHOR

Sally Morgan started writing when she was eight, but when *The Mystery of Adventure* did not become an overnight sensation, she abandoned her literary career and went off to collect snakes. It wasn't until after a painful mid-life divorce that she found herself, quite by accident, with a collection of men and a story that needed to be told. Sally lives in Victoria, BC with her husband and their boys. She is a teacher and writer, and you can find her at www.alphabetofmen.com. *An Alphabet of Men* is Sally's first book.

www.ingramcontent.com/pod-product-compliance
Lightning Source LLC
Chambersburg PA
CBHW021923040426
42448CB00008B/888
* 9 7 8 0 9 9 5 8 4 3 6 0 8 *